Teacher Handbooks Talking and Listening

General Editor David Wray

Published by Scholastic Publications Ltd,
Marlborough House, Holly Walk,
Leamington Spa, Warwickshire CV32 4LS

© 1990 Scholastic Publications Ltd.

Contributors: David Wray (General editor), Barrie
Wade, Sarah Tann, Terry Phillips, Margaret Armitage,
Clive Carré, Janet Duffin

Edited by Jackie Cunningham-Craig
Sub-edited by Catherine Baker
Illustrations on pages 29, 38, 150 and 151 by Chris
Saunderson
Photographs by :
Barnaby's Picture Library pages 32 and 82
Sally and Richard Greenhill pages 42, 81, 102 and 103
Times Newspapers Ltd page 63
Mary Evans Picture Library page 117
The Manzell Collection page 119
Dave Richardson pages 25, 27, 35, 36, 44, 52, 104, 139,
142, 146
Richard Butchins pages 6, 9, 16, 22, 26, 37, 41, 43, 47,
48, 49, 59, 60, 62, 75, 84, 85, 87, 91, 101, 107, 108, 109,
123, 124, 125, 126, 127, 128, 129, 130, 131, 132, 133, 134,
137, 138, 140, 141, 143, 145, 147, 148, 152, 153, 156, 157,
162
All other photographs by Isabelle Butchinsky
Front and back cover: photographs by Martyn
Chillmaid, designed by Sue Limb
Artwork by Liz Preece, Castle Graphics, Kenilworth
Designed using Aldus Pagemaker
Processed by Typesetters (Birmingham) Ltd, Warley,
West Midlands
Printed in Great Britain by Ebenezer Baylis, Worcester

Our thanks to the staff and children of Brookhurst
Combined School, Leamington Spa for all their help
and co-operation

British Library Cataloguing in Publication Data
Talking and Listening: teacher handbook.
    1. Children. Language skills
    I. Wray, David, *1950* -
    401.9

ISBN 0-590-76206-0

Contents

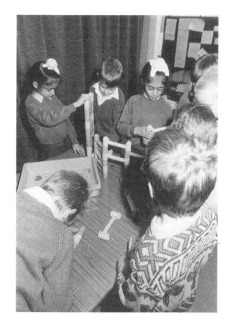

Contents

Introduction
David Wray

In the National Curriculum proposals for English (DES 1989) speaking and listening, for a long time neglected aspects in the teaching of English and language development generally, are given equal importance with the traditional first two Rs, reading and writing. In assessing children's achievements in English at ages seven and eleven all three Profile Components, reading, writing, and speaking and listening, are to be given equal weighting. In many respects this represents a considerable challenge to primary school teachers who, while generally running more talk-orientated classrooms, have in the main given little real concentration to the role and development of oracy in the classroom. This situation clearly has to change. By the age of eleven (Level 5 in National Curriculum terms) children will be expected to be able to:

• Give a well organised and sustained account of an event, a personal experience or an activity.
• Contribute to and respond constructively in discussion or debate, advocating and justifying a particular point of view.
• Use transactional language effectively in a straightforward situation.
• Plan and participate in a presentation.
• Talk about variations in vocabulary between different regional or social groups.

This will demand two important requirements from teachers. Firstly, that they have some understanding of how oracy develops, its role in learning, and possible strategies for assisting this development. Secondly, that teachers provide opportunities for children to develop their speaking and listening.

This book will be of great assistance, as it deals with many important issues; the role of talk in learning, the development of the ability to listen, language variation and children's awareness. Chapters have also been included which concentrate on practical suggestions for incorporating

productive talk into primary classrooms, in a variety of curriculum areas from science and mathematics to cross-curricular project work. Decisions about the provision of opportunities for the development of oracy can properly be made only by teachers themselves. *Teacher Handbooks Talking and Listening* gives many suggestions for the provision and structuring of these opportunities, but these will not be easy to provide. The major problem with a curriculum in which children achieve much of their learning through talking is that it produces classrooms which do not conform to many people's (teachers included) stereotypes of what a good classroom should be like. The picture of a 'good' classroom which most non-teachers and many teachers have is one where children get on with their work in as quiet an atmosphere as possible (they concentrate better that way), and if discussion takes place it is closely controlled by the teacher (who after all does know more than the children) and follows fairly tight rules (one person speaks at once, no interruptions, wait to be asked to speak by the teacher; these rules help develop 'civilised' behaviour). Most teachers, if they are honest, will admit to having had at some time a sneaking feeling that this is what their classroom should really be like. This feeling may have been endorsed by the reactions of their fellow-teachers who may have commented adversely on lively classroom discussions: 'Your lot were noisy this morning, Miss Smith. I nearly came in to give them a talking to, only I saw you were with them.'

This idea about classrooms holds the underlying view that talking is negative. Talk is unavoidable, but the less there is of it, the more real learning will take place. The

National Curriculum (and an almost overwhelming weight of evidence and theoretical argument) makes it essential that teachers give talk a more prominent role in their classrooms than before. This may well mean standing up strongly to doubters, and we hope that this book will be the source of some powerful ammunition in the fight.

Why talk?
Barrie Wade

Why talk?
Barrie Wade

INTRODUCTION

'Paul is very articulate,' said the class teacher approvingly at a parents' evening.

'Yes, he's always drawing at home,' Paul's mother replied.

'He's good at talking too,' continued the teacher.

Faced with this dialogue you will already have begun to interact with the text, to make sense of it, to think about it and relate its meaning to your own experiences. Is the written version an accurate record of what was spoken? What was said next? Is it true or is it made up? For the purposes of drawing attention to fundamental aspects of language I shall provide no answers!

These three questions are, however, important ones. We know that spoken language differs from writing in its form and in the way it is used. The listener can give feedback to the speaker in talk and the speaker can make immediate adjustments, as occurred in the example. Secondly, language occurs not in isolation but in a social context. To the teacher, communication of approval of Paul and maintaining the positive relationship with his mother is more important than teaching an adult a new word. Thirdly, in speaking and listening we actively monitor what both we and other people say in an effort to control what meanings are communicated and how they are interpreted. We all know that talk can be used to deceive as well as to inform. Although it is used to comment on the real world, language is an abstract system and meanings have to be wrestled with.

Paul may always be blissfully unaware of this talk about him, but the conversation draws our attention to the power of a language system. Talk (and writing, of course) frees us from the here-and-now, because we can talk meaningfully about things that are not actually present. This attribute is exclusively human. Parrots may mimic, apes may make signs that relate to objects, dogs may salivate at non-verbal signals such as a food cupboard door opening: but only human beings actively construct their representations of reality and communicate their meanings effectively in talk. The process begins very early on, as we can see from the following example of a girl (not quite 2) talking with her mother.

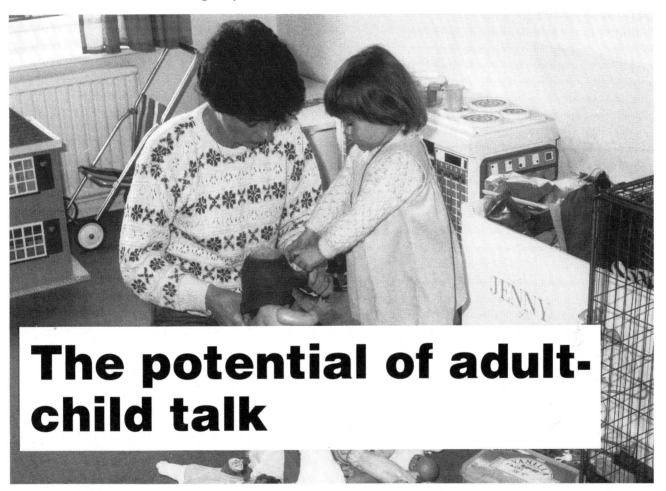

The potential of adult-child talk

Imogen, aged one year and ten months, has arranged her dolls around her and has called her mother for help:

1 Adult: What do you want me to fetch
2 Imogen: um/some toys for them
3 A: well you've got some there haven't you/you sort out what toys you want
4 I: I/I want two of them
5 A: choose
6 I: Mummy can you choose
7 A: well I don't know what sort of toys your babies will like/you have a look what's in there
8 I: yes
9 A: and in this box
10 I: oo/that I want/and that/my baby wants the ring/she wants this
11 A: oh
12 I: and she wants that/oh that's come out
13 A: oh has it
14 I: put it back in

15 A: I'll just pop it back/there we are/it's a bit big isn't it

16 I: mm

17 A: Whoops-a-daisy we've lost it haven't we/which way up does it go

18 I: don't know

19 A: shall we just put it in/I don't know how we're going to put it do you/stand up and I'll try and put it on/it's a funny old thing isn't it

20 I: oh/yes

21 A: which one do you think wants that one

22 I: um/baby Thomas/ you know

23 A: well/you'd better tell him what it is because he won't know

24 I: what/what it is/I've put him to bed

25 A: you've put him to bed/oh

26 I: whoops/whoops/sort some out/some more out/they want/tip some more out (mutters to herself) they want and that to share don't they/baby/baby Thomas can have the duck for a minute/have to share this/yes/and a teddy for that one/and

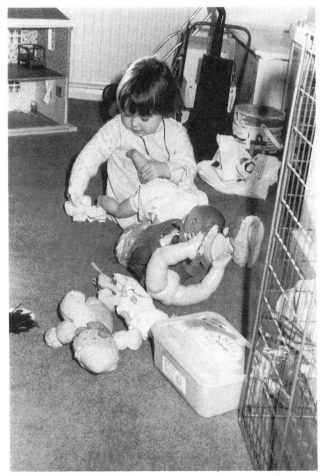

There are many opportunities for meaningful talk in play.

again a car for that one/a squeezy for that one/this one/oh the baby wants this one...

The conversation is relaxed and purposeful. Imogen deliberately involves her mother in conversation about the task as well as using talk to give a commentary on her own actions. From the early years talk is social and purposeful. Parents intuitively know that if they encourage meaningful conversations, children will find language appropriate for their needs and will learn through trying things out in talk. The adult constantly encourages both her child's activity (3, 5, 7) and her conversational responses (15, 17, 19) by appropriate questions. It is clear that the child is far from a passive learner of language; she takes an equal and active part in the talk, taking initiative (10), giving instructions (14), and asserting her needs (4). Already she has mastered the pattern of conversation: pausing to listen, taking her turn, taking and surrendering initiative. Observation of babies teaches us that this turn-taking is learned from the earliest weeks of life. Indeed, the framework of a relaxed conversation is necessary to put language to use for learning purposes. Notice how Imogen is confident enough to try out (26) 'whoops/whoops/sort some out/some more out' - some of the terms her mother had used earlier (3 and 17). She also experiments successfully with the concept of sharing toys as she distributes them between her dolls. This kind of reconstruction and recreation is a feature of relaxed talk and leads to learning.

Adults provide models for children to learn to talk and to learn through talking, but it is important to remember that modelling does not simply mean child imitating adult. Indeed the only example of direct imitation in the example given occurs in 24 and 25 where her mother follows Imogen's pattern. Language learning is much more than a matter of transmission of information or direct imitation.

Our next example shows the tremendous amount of practice and learning which goes on when children play together. It reveals the potential for effective group talk in classrooms.

The potential of child-child talk

Two children, R and M, are playing outside near a swing. R, aged three years and five months, wants to swing, but is persuaded to be a shopkeeper by M, aged two years and four months, so that M can be a shopper.

1 R: can I have a swing later/will you/ don't push me/what do you want/put your basket on the floor/put it on the floor/what do you want
2 M: er some/some
3 R: some nothing milk (she offers empty Chocolate Whip packet)
4 M: no/some liquid/liquid/how much is it
5 R: ten and a pound
6 M: can I (have) that (taking empty washing-up liquid container)
7 R: what else do you want/some liquid
8 M: I've got some liquid
9 R: squeeze it
10 M: it won't come out
11 R: shall I show you how it goes it goes (takes container and squeezes it hard) like that (bubbles appear) that's it/look/a bubble
12 M: I want some/vitamin drops/how much is this vitamin drops
13 R: er/ten

14 M: (Indecipherably) how much is
15 R: (Continuing to squeeze container) look some bubbles coming/look
16 M: how much is this soap
17 R: er/it's ten
18 M: can I have this (taking large empty salt container)
19 R: no you can't/put it back until you've had the little things/what else do you want to buy
20 M: some/some soap
21 R: this is laughing salt would you like laughing salt - would you like some dinner (pointing out several pans)
22 M: like some dinner
23 R: what sort of dinner this (packet)
24 M: I want diller (dinner?)
25 R: no you can't have diller/do you want this diller/do you want that dinner
26 M: yes I do/put it in my basket
27 R: say how pound is it
28 M: how pound is it
29 R: it's four and a twenty half

One way of assessing the value of this kind of conversation is to examine the purposes involved in the talk, how they relate to the speakers themselves and what indications we have that learning is taking

Children can learn very early on to be persuasive.

Talk to express need

A central function of talk for the individual is the establishment of personal desires, wants and needs, whether expressed as a declaration: 'I want some/vitamin drops'(12) or as part of negotiations: 'can I have a swing later'(1).

Talk to control others

Teachers and parents know that messages can only be delivered when attention is well-directed and behaviour is controlled. Young children learn this too: eg 'don't push me'(1).

Control systems can be invented or changed in the process of talk, as we regularly see in interviews given by politicians! No supermarket that I know insists shoppers purchase small items first, but R stops the purchase of a large item : 'no you can't/put it back until you've had the little things'(19).

Talk to maintain relationships

A crucial function of talk is to build and maintain relationships. We know, for example, that unless people can co-operate socially they are unlikely to make progress on collaborative tasks. R encourages conversation; for example, 'what else do you want to buy'(19), 'would you like some dinner'(21), and she offers help: 'shall I show you how it goes' (11) M asks before taking the washing-up liquid container: 'can I (have) that' (6).

Part of sustaining a relationship is using language reciprocally. For example, we shift our accents when we return to parts of a country that we used to live in and take up relationships there. R has probably never heard the made-up word 'diller' before, yet she uses it ('do you want this diller'(25)) to maintain their relationship and their roles.

place. This assessment, as with all uses of language, involves interpretation, but the functions of talk in the example include the following.

Talk for role-play

Both children use talk to develop their roles of shopkeeper and shopper. The need to operate in these roles causes them to seek for appropriate language: eg 'what do you want' (1) 'how much is this soap' (16)

Talk to accompany action

We frequently use language to demonstrate a process or as a commentary. The children show they can link talk to actions: 'it won't come out' (10), 'it goes like that that's it/look/a bubble' (11).

Talk to give directions

The directions we give to others are part of our need to control their behaviour; they also ensure that our conversations proceed appropriately according to experience as we know it. R directs M to act like the shoppers she has observed: 'put your basket on the floor' (1) M directs R to act like the shopkeepers she has observed: 'put it in my basket' (26).

Talk to convey information

Most adults, when asked what language is used for, would answer that it is used to communicate information to others. Children employ this function; for example, 'this is laughing salt' (21), 'it's four and a twenty half' (29), but they use many others as well.

Talk for finding out

When we want to know something we usually ask, for questioning is fundamental to the inquiry and discovery that make the learning process an active one. These children already understand that questioning produces information; for example, 'what do you want' (1) 'how much is it'(4).

Children soon learn that talk can convey many different meanings.

Talk for imaginative purposes

Sometimes when lost for words we speak of 'thingummies' or 'whatsits' to avoid blanks in our conversations. These children avoid gaps by constructing meanings that have more significance than such clichés: 'nothing milk'(3) is an empty packet; 'laughing salt'(21) is a brand of salt with a broadly smiling face on the packet. We can see that M uses the world 'diller' as a variation on 'dinner' in response to the question 'what sort of dinner'(23). Without the transcript we might have thought the two-year-old could not say 'dinner'; in fact, she has already used it correctly.

It is clear from this brief analysis of some of the main functions of language that young children learn to use talk for various purposes very early on. Different authorities have constructed their own differing lists of language functions, (see for example, M A K Halliday and Joan Tough in B Wade, 1982). It is unlikely that we shall ever have a single, agreed model of language functions, but there is agreement that this early learning of language for different purposes puts the child on the road to learning. Using language to discover information, for imaginative purposes, or for exploring a role, for example, are important processes in education. Classrooms must offer children the opportunity to practise language for the range of purposes that they have developed naturally, instead of merely emphasising teacher-talk for giving information.

An important part of learning is using language to practise roles and to clarify ideas, as these children do. They have observed real shopping. Talk now gives them the opportunity to practise the observed roles and to make sense of past experiences. The nature of their conversation gives purpose to their activity and allows them to learn and to experiment with words such as 'liquid' and 'vitamin' and structures such as 'how pound is it' (28). This is similar to the argument made elsewhere (Wade, 1989) that reading should be encouraged to develop from whole, meaningful stories, rather than from sounds or isolated words tacked together.

Learning through talk

The importance of anecdote

The following conversation took place in a primary school between a teacher and Alison, aged seven; it corresponds to the natural conversations between parents and children that we discussed previously (see page 11). However, as it takes place in school, we shall evaluate it as a learning experience.

1 Alison: we've got a lot of cats around/I don't know why it's always the same cat/a black cat/there's a black cat/a tom cat, and they're all prowling around/and er/what
2 Adult: do you think they're after the robin
3 Alison: well/no/they're not after the robin they're after the pigeons/a cat can tell/me dad he flies pigeons and we have a club/and we go there Friday night have a drink and then go/um/this pigeon he was/we've got a great big field and they were settling on it/ooh dad was ever so proud of it/it er/it had won him a lot of money/well/me dad he/the loft's here and the grass's thick and me dad was scraping out/the er/pigeon loft and this cat it got/it knew which bird er won it/he got it and me dad he was/he looked round and said where's the one that won me this money and it had gone/and the other time
4 Adult: had the cat got it then
5 Alison: it had got it
6 Adult: how do you think it knew which one to go for
7 Alison: well/you see/every/every bird had got a ring mark on/we found out that some/somehow the cats know which ring mark to go to/um/before they're put in the crates and sent to where they're going/to be flown back home/its/who/whose per/whose person's pigeon come back the first will get a prize/um/another time um/when it's put on/when/before it goes in the crate there's a/a ring mark put on/um they put a rubber ring on so/you see/if it comes in you must put the rubber ring in a thimble/put it in the master timer and that/that brings out the clock times/time er
8 Adult: you think that the cat learned that did it

9 Alison: he knows which ring marks?

We can see from the conversational pattern that Alison takes an active, initiatory part in the talk. Her teacher listens willingly and interestedly, giving Alison the chance to shape her story and to order her experience. The child is allowed to talk in the role of expert because she has selected a subject she knows more about than her teacher. Notice the way the teacher values her contribution, giving her the confidence to make concepts explicit (for example, her explanation of timing pigeons), and also encourages her to tackle awkward structures: 'who/whose/whose person's pigeon'(7).

Anecdotes like this offer practice in using language and in developing the functions that were discussed on page 12. Alison takes the opportunity to explain, to narrate, to shape her story effectively, to maintain the relationship with her listener and to clarify events for her own understanding. This last function is an

One child's experience of pigeons offers practice in using language.

important one, for talk allows us the chance to make meaning and to develop understanding through the actual process of talking. The puzzle for Alison possibly stems from some strong remark her father made about the predatory cat which seemed to know which were the best birds. In trying to solve the puzzle of how the cat knew she uses the talk just as much for her own clarification as for giving information to her teacher. Notice how she develops her ideas about the cat and in this short extract has at least five attempts to state its deliberate intention and how it knew which pigeon to kill: 'I don't know why it's always the same cat/a black cat'(1), 'a cat can tell'(3), 'this cat it got/it knew which bird er won it'(3), 'somehow the cats know which ring mark to go to'(7), 'he knows which ring marks'(9).

Alison makes connections between her knowledge of how adults identify pigeons and the event she narrates. In this way she uses the chance of talking to speculate, to hypothesise and to clarify and formulate her meaning. Of course, there are bound to be wrong turnings, corrections and restatements in the process. Importantly, exploratory talk of this kind gives the opportunity for insight, self-correction, discovery and refinement of thinking during the process of talking. Anecdotes therefore allow the active reorganisation of what a learner has experienced, and this reordering through talking is an important part of learning.

It is essential for teachers to recognise that the power of talk to aid learning can be encouraged in a cross-curricular project, and should not merely be limited to a pupil's own experience. Exploratory talk can be used to order information and to make sense of other people's experiences, for example.

The importance of cross-curricular talk

The pupils in this final example are both nine years old. Their class is engaged on the topic of Captain Cook's voyages. They have seen a film and have read several documents and historical accounts with details of geographical and botanical discovery. Their class teacher's intention is that each pupil should write an account of life on board the Endeavour as a way of empathising with Cook's ordinary seamen as well as ordering some of the available information. Moving from facts to an abstract written version is a large jump for many children, so she first sets up work where pupils interview each other and thus gain practice at taking a role. The children talk in pairs simultaneously, one taking the role of an able seaman, the other that of a BBC reporter.

1 Rachel: when you got to/Botany Bay/ were there really so many strange plants and/what were their names like/
2 Andrea: oh no (under breath) there was lots of strange plants indeed but I couldn't remember a single name/lots of them were named after Mr Banks/
3 Rachel: and he was one of the botanists you say/
4 A: yes/
5 R: when you got to/er/the/north from Botany Bay/were you grounded on some/ sharp rock or something/
6 A: yes it was coral actually a coral reef/ called the Great Barrier Reef/
7 R: was it/frightening/
8 A: well/it was in a way yes/
9 R: and you say/Cook Town where you landed and repaired the ship/was it good ground?/
10 A: yes very/
11 R: we were told that the captain/um/ planted the British flag/
12 A: yes he did/Captain Cook/
13 R: and/er/did you ever think that you wouldn't get home/back/
14 A: yes/most of the time I did yes/
15 R: what about leaving your family/you have a family/and children/
16 A: um/well I'm a sailor/sailors have do things like that/
17 R: yes I suppose it comes with the job/ what happened if you didn't eat this/ sauerkraut/
18 A: well/two of my mates didn't eat the

Interviewing gives practice in role-playing.

sauerkraut/they absolutely detested it/and they threw it overboard/so/a board was put up/on deck/it was a wooden board with holes in/everyone was made to watch/and my mates' shirts were taken off/and then they were strapped by their ankles/and wrists to the board/and while the drum/the drummer played a silent drum/they were whipped/twelve times/
19 R: and after that/did you eat the sauer kraut/
20 A: well Captain Cook decided whipping wasn't the right thing to do/and he said if we didn't want it we didn't have to/eat it/but the officers still had it/so we decided if the officers could have it/we should be able to have it/and we ate so much eventually/that it had to be rationed/
21 R: oh/er/ (pause) this was the BBC news reporter.

By taking these roles the participants are encouraged to find the language appropriate for the subject, the purpose and the listener. Naturally it takes pupils some time and some experimentation to discover the appropriate language forms for unfamiliar points of view. To begin with Rachel gives information rather than eliciting it (1, 3, 5, 6, 9, 11) as she takes on the role of interviewer. Andrea is limited by the questions and, just as pupils are when teachers ask closed questions, she is driven to provide short answers (4, 6, 8, 10, 12). More importantly, as well as exchanging and ordering information, the girls are learning through talk how to conduct an interview. Rachel learns to ask more open questions (17 and 19) and these draw longer, more detailed (and more interesting) responses from Andrea (18 and 20). The passage dramatically shows how the quality of talk depends on all participants and how teachers need to consider their own input when evaluating pupils' performance.

Talk does not exist in isolation. We have already explored the links between experience and talk, and those between drama or role-play and talk. Talk can also be used as a rehearsal for writing - a kind of spoken first draft before pen is put to paper. The quality of Andrea's work may be judged from her writing which follows:

Life on Board the Endeavour
Before we set sail all sorts of things were brought on board such as chickens, beef, pigs, some fresh vegetables, pickled cabbage, lots of scientific equipment and of course rum and wine. We had to wait for a while before we set sail because some rich person was late and Captain Cook wouldn't let us sail without him. He arrived with two greyhounds. I feel a bit sorry for the dogs because they won't have a good run around on board.

We had a mixture of weather. Sometimes it snowed or rained and other times the sun shone. We were freezing sometimes at night. We were told the rules then set to work. Some men washed the animals or scrubbed the decks with water and scrubbing stones. But I didn't do any of those jobs instead I had to clean the wood in our living quarters with gunpowder and vinegar and did it smell horrible!

For nearly every meal we had pickled cabbage and not surprisingly some of my mates got fed up of it and refused to eat it. So a wooden board was put up which had holes in and my mates' shirts were taken off before they were tied by their wrists and ankles to the board. Everyone was made to watch and while they were being whipped somebody played a drum very slowly. My mate said the whipping was painful but Captain Cook had decided whipping was the wrong thing to do and he told us that if we didn't want it we didn't have to eat the pickled cabbage if we did eat it that was alright but the officers still had pickled cabbage so we want it and soon we ate so much it had to be rationed.

The quality of children's work is greatly enhanced through the experience of role-play.

At night we were cramped together. We had a 5 foot by 14 inch hammock and it wasn't at all comfortable.

After about 4 months we reached Georges Island. It was great lots of fresh food and lots of space to move around in. Most of us sailors were trading nails and beads. When I was walking around on the island I noticed 2 natives tatooing themselves with sharpened bones. While we were on the island one of the artists or botanists died. I'm not sure which he was.

When the officers had seen Venus pass the sun we set sail for the new continent. We were attacked not far from land by fierce natives. So we sailed away from the land.

We landed on an island which was claimed for Britain and the Captain called the land around, New South Wales and the place we landed on was called Botany Bay because there was lots of new plants growing there. Most of them had been eventually named after Mr Banks the botanist. The soil in Botany Bay was fertile and rich. We left Botany Bay after the botanists ahd collected and pressed all they wanted and the artists had painted all they wanted.

We were sailing along when suddenly we jolted to a stop. My mates and I rushed on board deck to see what had happened. Captain Cook rushed out of his cabin and told us we were stuck on a coal reef. He ordered us to throw empty barrels overboard in hope of floating away and then he ordered some of us to start the pumps going to get the water out. We ran out of empty barrels so we started to throw the guns overboard. Then I threw out the anchor at Captain's order. Then every free hand was used to pull in the anchor. We did this in hope of pulling the boat towards the anchor. After 23 hours we managed to free the ship from the coral. We sailed on and came to some land which we named after the Captain. Cook Town was its name and when we got there we found 2 large bits of coral covering the hole.

The usefulness of talk as a way into writing may be seen from the way Andrea has such a firm grasp of the information she conveys and of the point of view from which she conveys it. Details such as: 'while they were being whipped somebody played a drum very slowly' have been clarified from the spoken version: while the drum/ the drummer played a silent drum (18).

Because there are inherent connections between experience, listening, talking, reading and writing, good talk is one helpful route towards good writing in all areas of the curriculum.

In this chapter talk has been shown as a method of learning as well as a way of communicating. By examining examples of children and adults talking, the hesitancy, tentativeness and shifts of direction which are features of exploratory talk have been revealed. The examination of evidence, speculation, formulation of ideas and self-correction that ensue when learners try out in dialogue thoughts which otherwise would remain unclarified for the speaker and unknown to the listener have also been

Interviewing and role-play will bring to life what it was like on board the Endeavour.

shown. Once thoughts are made public through talk, speaker and listener can reflect about them, criticise them, alter them and refine them, achieving both learning and a greater control over thinking. The implication is that in school talk must become a centrally important contribution to learning. Teachers must encourage effective talk in pairs, groups and in class, they must give real point and purpose to pupils' talk and encourage a collaborative, open and trusting approach. They must become good listeners too. It has been argued (Moffett, 1968) that the dialogues we engage in determine our abilities in thinking.

Teachers can take heart from the main direction of recent proposals for attainment targets in different areas of the National Curriculum. Emphasis is placed upon the active processes of learning and upon the meanings and understandings to be generated through sharing and interacting.

Speaking and listening have been presented as just as important as writing and reading, and their relationship to learning has been emphasised by the National Curriculum English Working Group:
'Our inclusion of speaking and listening as a separate profile component in our recommendations is a reflection of our conviction that they are of central importance to children's development.' There is, of course, a difference between making the case for talk and instituting change at a classroom level. Other chapters in this book offer guidance for developing this good practice into a rich harvest.

Teachers should encourage effective talk in pairs.

Acknowledgements

The transcript in Section 4(a) is part of a longer conversation analysed in *Talking to Some Purpose* ed B Wade (1985) Educational Review Publications, University of Birmingham.

Although it is treated differently here, acknowledgement is made to the board of editors *Educational Review*.

Language variation
David Wray

Language variation
David Wray

INTRODUCTION

In the United Kingdom the language used in the majority of our public institutions is almost exclusively Standard English. This form of the language dominates the media, from newspapers to television; public proceedings are conducted in it, from legal to political in most cases; and education is dominated by it, from universities to primary schools. It is, therefore, very easy to make the assumption that the United Kingdom is a linguistically homogeneous country. This is, however, far from the truth. The majority of the population do not, in fact, use Standard English as their most common form of spoken language, and in certain areas of the country there are many schools where a significant proportion of the children do not use English at all as their first language when at home with their parents.

Diversity of language is a fact of life and teachers need to take it into account when responding to and developing the linguistic competence of pupils. To do this teachers need firstly to understand language variation. In what ways does language vary within Britain, and within English itself? Secondly teachers need to work out their positions on the issues which stem from this variation. If there is such variation within language, is it sensible to talk about 'correct' forms of language? If children do not have full mastery of particular forms are they by that token linguistically deprived?

Forms of variation

Language varies in four major ways. Firstly, and most obviously, there is the variation between different languages as, for example, between Greek and Gujurati. It is quite common, and in some areas normal, for teachers in primary schools to have to deal with children who speak languages other than English at home.

Secondly, there are variations due to dialect. A speaker from Northumberland will use some different words and some different language structures from those used by a speaker from Liverpool. Teachers will often not converse naturally in the same dialect as the children they teach, and this can sometimes cause problems.

Thirdly, speakers may differ in accent, ie the way words are pronounced. A speaker from Northumberland may use exactly the same words and structures as a Londoner, but still have problems making himself understood because of accent differences.

Finally, and perhaps most commonly, language may vary in terms of register. We use different styles of speaking in formal situations and in informal, often choosing different words or expressions as well as varying in pace and articulation.

Languages

It is quite surprising to realise the range of different languages spoken by inhabitants of the United Kingdom. Although a complete national picture is difficult to come by, such surveys that do exist suggest an extremely complex picture. The ILEA language census, for example, announced in 1983 that 147 different languages were used by children who were at that time in London schools!

Many children will, of course, speak more than one or two languages. It is quite remarkable that some young children can cope with the range of languages they have to contend with. Consider, for example, eight-year-olds who were found in a primary school in Cardiff. These children were of Pakistani origin and spoke Gujurati at home and with some of their friends. On occasions at home, and at Saturday school, they learnt and spoke Urdu. They were also learning Arabic for religious purposes, although this was not used conversationally. At school they used English in class and with some of their friends, but, because they were attending a bi-lingual school, in class they were also learning and speaking Welsh.

This range is surprising enough in itself, but what is even more remarkable is that these children did not appear to be suffering from any emotional traumas because of their linguistic situation, and neither did there seem to be much interference of one language with another. They rarely mixed the languages they were using, mainly because each had a quite tightly defined social context in which it was acceptable or expected.

Of course, this range of language experience is not common. Many children do, however, cope with two distinct languages on an everyday basis. Schools often perceive this as a problem, although it has to be remarked that this is sometimes a differential perception. Children who are reasonably fluent in English, French and German, say, are usually thought of as quite clever, although the same label is often not applied to children who are reasonably fluent in English, Punjabi and Urdu, or English, Marathi and Hindi. Children who cope with a range of linguistic demands ought really to be given credit for their efforts.

The pattern of language use varies across the country. This can be easily seen by looking at some extracts from the information revealed by the Linguistic Minorities Project in 1983. Children in school in various education authorities were asked if they spoke a language other than English at home, and what it was.

In Bradford out of 79,758 pupils that were surveyed in the age range six to 16, 17.8% claimed to speak a language other than English at home. The most popular languages mentioned were Punjabi (by 52.7% of those who did claim to speak another language), Urdu (19%) and Gujurati (8.8%).

In Peterborough 32,662 pupils were surveyed in the age range five to 16 and 7.4% claimed to speak a language other than English at home. The most popular languages mentioned were Punjabi (24%), Italian (23.7%), Urdu (17.8%) and Gujurati (11.5%)

In Haringey 24,140 pupils were surveyed in the age range five to 15 and 30.7% claimed to speak a language other than English at home. The most popular languages mentioned were Greek (34.1%), Turkish (14.7%) and English-based Creoles (9.3%).

These differential patterns, of course, represent different immigration and settlement histories, but they also give rise to some interesting points. Firstly the figures may be somewhat surprising in that they may not accord with some popular impressions derived from the media. They warn us against making easy assumptions. Secondly they suggest that part of the task of teachers should be actually to find out what the linguistic composition of their classes and schools may be. It is difficult to plan for effective development without this information. Lack of information may lead to under-estimation on the part of teachers, and the self-fulfilling prophecies which often stem from labelling.

Dialects

There are many regional variations within English itself and these dialects differ from one another in terms of the vocabulary and the grammatical structures they employ. Vocabulary differences caused by dialect can be a source of some confusion, but also a great deal of amusement.

Take the following words: stream, brook, beck, burn. One of these is likely to be the natural word you use to refer to a small river, but if you use your word in an area where the dialect term is different you are likely to cause some confusion and be thought of as 'posh' or just strange. There are many examples like this. Some dialect terms are in fact more straightforward in their derivation than those used in the Standard English dialect. The Lancashire word 'childer', for example, is a logical development of the Old English plural form. 'Children' is, in fact, a double plural. Of course, the North-East England form 'bairns', and the West Scotland form 'weans' are derivations from different roots.

A favourite dialect vocabulary variant is the word used for the soft, usually white,

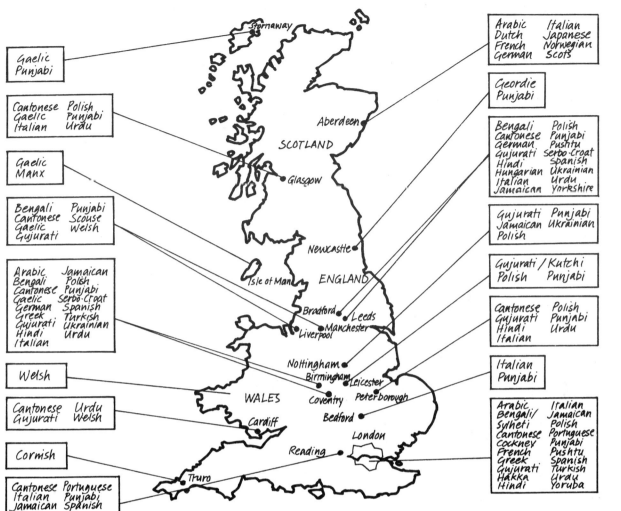

Gaelic
Punjabi

Cantonese Polish
Gaelic   Punjabi
Italian   Urdu

Gaelic
Manx

Bengali   Punjabi
Cantonese   Scouse
Gaelic   Welsh
Gujurati

Arabic   Jamaican
Bengali   Polish
Cantonese   Punjabi
Gaelic   Serbo-Croat
German   Spanish
Greek   Turkish
Gujurati   Ukrainian
Hindi   Urdu
Italian

Welsh

Cantonese   Urdu
Gujurati   Welsh

Cornish

Cantonese   Portuguese
Italian   Punjabi
Jamaican   Spanish

Arabic   Italian
Dutch   Japanese
French   Norwegian
German   Scots

Geordie
Punjabi

Bengali   Polish
Cantonese   Punjabi
German   Pushtu
Gujurati   Serbo-Croat
Hindi   Spanish
Hungarian   Ukrainian
Italian   Urdu
Jamaican   Yorkshire

Gujurati   Punjabi
Jamaican   Ukrainian
Polish

Gujurati / Kutchi
Polish   Punjabi

Cantonese   Polish
Gujurati   Punjabi
Hindi   Urdu
Italian

Italian
Punjabi

Arabic   Italian
Bengali/   Jamaican
Sylheti   Polish
Cantonese   Portuguese
Cockney   Punjabi
French   Pushtu
Greek   Spanish
Gujurati   Turkish
Hakka   Urdu
Hindi   Yoruba

Stornaway
Aberdeen
SCOTLAND
Glasgow
Newcastle
Isle of Man
ENGLAND
Bradford Leeds
Liverpool Manchester
Nottingham
Birmingham Leicester
Coventry Peterborough
WALES Bedford
Cardiff
London
Reading
Truro

This map shows you some of the languages spoken in different parts of Britain.
Look on it to find the town or city nearest to where you live. See how many languages are spoken there.
Are there any languages spoken by pupils in your class that are not mentioned on the map?
If so, add them to the list.

shoes that children wear on their feet for indoor physical education. In the South-East these are called plimsolls, in the North-East, sandshoes, in the South-West, daps, and the North-West, pumps. There may be many other variations. In Barrow-in-Furness, for example, children refer to these as 'galoshes', a word which has a completely different meaning elsewhere in the country. Increasingly the words 'trainers' and 'sneakers' are also used for these shoes. This is, of course, vital information for teachers, many of whom must have experienced the bemused reactions of their classes when asked to get out their plimsolls/pumps/daps etc when this was not the children's word!

Dialects also differ in terms of their grammatical structure. These structures can be so much a part of our everyday speech it can be difficult to recognise them as dialect variants.

For example, each of the following versions are acceptable in one of the dialects spoken widely in Britain.

This is the boy what did it.
This is the boy which did it.
This is the boy that did it.
This is the boy as did it.
This is the boy at did it.
This is the boy did it.

Dialect grammatical forms tend to vary in several ways in addition to the differing use of relative pronouns described. Some dialects use verb forms such as: 'I goes, you goes, he goes, we goes, they goes'. Others use: 'I go, you go, he go, we go, they go'.

Many dialects use multiple negatives such as 'I didn't get nothing'. Others regularly use 'ain't' or 'never' as a negative form, for example 'It ain't there' or 'I never done it'. Standard English 'those' is often replaced, for example, 'Give me they pliers'.

The important thing to note about these forms is that they are regular and consistent, not haphazard and sloppy uses of English. It therefore would be inappropriate for a teacher to admonish a child who uses these forms for simply being 'wrong'. In the child's terms, these forms are 'right', because these are what he hears at home and consistently uses. There might be occasions when these forms are not appropriate, and it is this sense of appropriateness which the teacher needs to help children develop.

The fact is that all speakers of English employ a dialect of some kind. Standard English itself is a dialect, having developed from the dialect spoken around the administrative centre of the country in medieval times. Because of increasing centralisation this dialect became more and more important until eventually it was accepted as the English dialect.

Standard English used to be the form that was taught as 'English' to non-English speakers, although there has been a notable change in this in recent years, and learners of English are now more likely to be taught Standard American-English. This change emphasises the fact that Standard English is a dialect itself, and a Standard English speaker may well find his speech being questioned when talking to American English speakers.

There are, of course, many occasions when Standard English is the most appropriate form to use, and native English speakers accept this and generally comply. There are also, however, occasions when to use Standard English would be considered 'posh', or patronising and other dialects are more appropriate.

Accents

'Accent' refers to variations in language due to pronunciation. Accents may be associated with particular dialects, but this is not necessarily the case. A speaker from Edinburgh and a speaker from Hereford may both use Standard English, but pronounce their words in different ways. It is probably true to say that differences between regional dialects have declined over the past 100 years, but accent differences show no sign of diminishing. Indeed, it is much more common for people in public life to use a regional accent than it was 30 or 40 years ago. Most of us today find the accent used as standard in films and newsreels of the 1930s and 1940s rather strange. Accent has become a point of pride for many people, perhaps because it is an obvious means of signalling one's 'roots'.

It is still true, however, that different accents are perceived differently by people. The most prestigious is that known as Received Pronunciation, or RP, an extreme form of which is spoken by members of the Royal family. It is like Standard English, although in fact it is spoken naturally by relatively few people. It is not a regional accent but is associated rather with social

Standard-English found in dictionaries is itself a dialect.

Received Pronunciation can be found in positions of high status like judges and lawyers.

On the other hand, a speaker whose accent becomes more distinct from that of a listener may want a distancing from that person. The listener may interpret that as rejection. All these effects may vary depending upon the perceived status of speaker and listener.

Teachers need to be aware of the characteristics of their pupils' accents. This is necessary for effective communication, but it may also help explain some of the difficulties children may have. To take a simple example, a teacher with a South-Eastern accent needs to know that her Northern pupils may have difficulty distinguishing between her pronunciation of 'cup' and 'cap'. In their accent these two words will be pronounced completely differently and will never be confused.

Sometimes a teacher's ignorance of her pupils' accents may lead to incorrect judgements about their abilities. For example, a teacher in a school in Reading whose pupil wrote a poem in which he tried to rhyme the words 'spell', 'shall' and 'owl', might have thought this child did not

class. Its high status stems from this. Experiments have suggested, however, that this status is specific rather than general. These experiments have involved subjects listening to a speech given in a particular accent and then being asked to rate the speech and the speaker. The content of the speech was kept the same. Speakers who used RP were rated highly for competence, intelligence and industriousness, but regional accent speakers were rated more highly for integrity, sincerity and good-naturedness. Many politicians use effects like this to good advantage.

Most speakers are not consistent in their use of accent and vary their accent slightly, albeit subconsciously, depending upon who they are speaking to. This may involve the accent becoming more like that of the person being addressed, or less like it, and both of these shifts may have subtle intentions and effects. A speaker whose accent becomes closer to that of a listener may want a closer identification with that person. The listener may interpret the change as an attempt at friendliness and welcome it, or as patronising and reject it.

A teacher's accent can cause difficulties in class.

understand rhyming if she had not known that in a Reading accent these words do rhyme.

Teachers, of course, will have their own accents which may differ from those of their pupils. In rare cases, they may need to try to modify these slightly if they cause great communication problems in the classroom. More usually, however, a teacher's accent can be a useful idiosyncrasy which can help create a productive relationship with a class, and teachers should not feel that they have to make strenuous efforts to 'speak like the children'. This accent shifting could be interpreted as patronising, which will not help the teacher-pupil relationship at all.

Register

The final form of language variation is the most common of all. All of us make changes to the way we speak depending upon the social situation in which we find ourselves. We have several registers of language open to us and choose between them to suit a particular social context. These contexts vary chiefly in their degree of formality. When we visit a solicitor, for example, we are likely to use a different register of language than when we are relaxing with our friends. The language we use in these situations will vary in several ways:

- vocabulary - we are more likely to use slang expressions, or word approximations, such as 'thingummy' in informal contexts.
- syntax - in formal situations we are more likely to use Standard English forms, whereas in informal situations we will probably use such forms as contractions ('can't', 'innit'), incomplete sentences, and dialect structures.
- pace - in informal situations we tend to speak fairly quickly, whereas in formal contexts we generally use a more measured pace.

There is also variety between the registers we use for different informal contexts. We are likely to speak a little differently when we are with our families than with our closest friends. Similarly with formal contexts, the register we use when

We are likely to use a different register of language when we are in a more formal situation such as a job interview.

we wish to give a good impression, for example, in a job interview, will be slightly different from that we use in, say, a staff meeting.

The matching of register to situation is something most of us do without really thinking about it. We simply use language in the way which 'feels right'. This ability to sense appropriateness is, however, learned from experience, so we would expect children with more limited experience to be less skilled at it. One of the tasks of the teacher is to ensure that children are introduced to a broad enough range of social contexts, and given sufficient guidance for them to be able to learn to adapt their speech registers appropriately.

A further point arising from the language register/social situation link is that of 'correctness'. It would clearly be as incorrect to use a formal way of speaking in an informal situation as vice versa. The 'correct' way of speaking is that which is appropriate to the situation.

Issues arising from variation

Is one variety superior to another?

We have seen that there are wide variations between the forms of English, so it follows that when people talk about 'correct' English, they are implying that there is one form which is inherently superior to all others. This form is usually Standard English, which is also known as 'Oxford English', 'BBC English', or, most tellingly, 'Queen's English'.

Arguments for this superiority usually take two lines. One is to link 'correct' speech with clear, logical thinking, and conversely, non-standard, 'sloppy' speech with illogical thinking. A second argument is that of social currency. Because Standard English can be universally understood it is far more useful than regional dialects which are often difficult to understand outside their own regions.

Linguists have demonstrated beyond

dispute that all language varieties are rule-governed and consistent systems. The idea that dialect speech is simply sloppy, or a corruption of Standard English, is negated by this fact. There is therefore little substance to the argument that non-standard speech indicates illogical thought. Non-standard speech is just as logical as Standard English. It has also been shown that non-standard speakers are quite capable of logical reasoning, and nothing about their language holds them back. It is true, however, that some people, many teachers included, seem to believe that because children speak in a non-standard way, they have difficulties with logical thought. It is the perception of non-standard speech which is the problem, rather than its reality. Also language is not static, but constantly changing. Many language forms which would have been considered wrong 20 years ago are now in common use. If you look at the sentences below, each breaks a grammatical rule which I can remember being drilled in during my school days more than 20 years ago. An explanation of these rules can be found at the end of this chapter. You will probably agree, however, that these forms are inoffensive today.

1 Competitors should try and arrive in good time.
2 Who did you give the book to?
3 Everyone has their weaknesses.
4 He was better at it than me.
5 She did it quicker than usual.
6 It is hard to even think of that.
7 This is something I cannot deal with.

The second argument has more force. It is true that to succeed in modern society, a person needs to have command of Standard English, because, as already mentioned, all the institutions of society rely upon it. At some point in schooling, therefore, children need to be taught to use Standard English. There are several reservations to this argument, however.

Firstly, Standard English is first and foremost a written form of language. Although there are occasions when the spoken form is required, the main emphasis in schools should be upon children's ability to write Standard English. The recommendations of the National Curriculum support this by stating that primary school children should learn to produce and understand written Standard English, but only to understand the spoken form.

Secondly, and perhaps most importantly, developing a command of Standard English does not imply a denigration of the language variety children bring from home. The language people speak is closely linked with their identity, and to give them the message that their language is inadequate or inferior is to imply that they themselves are inferior. The alienation caused by this view is obvious. Children need to know that their natural language varieties are equal to but different from Standard English. 'No child should be expected to cast off the language and culture of the home as he crosses the school threshold.' (The Bullock Report, 1975).

There are occasions, however, when the use of Standard English would in fact be incorrect. A more useful concept to apply to language is that of appropriateness. The really skilful language users are those who can choose the appropriate dialect or register for the situation. This implies that part of the school's job is to develop children's ability to use language effectively in all situations, from streets and shops to courts and town halls. Developing this language awareness seems a far richer goal for schools than the narrow aim of teaching the use of Standard English.

Language deprivation

It has been consistently demonstrated that there is a link between social class and educational achievement. Middle class children achieve more than working class children at all levels of the educational system. The reasons for this situation have been under investigation for many years. Twenty years ago the idea emerged that the chief reason for the under-achievement of working class children might be their lack of command of the language forms necessary to succeed in school. The ideas of the sociologist, Basil Bernstein, were taken as support for this explanation. Bernstein claimed that there existed two distinct language codes. One, the restricted code, was characterised by short sentences, lack of adjectives and adverbs and a dependence upon the immediate context for its understanding. The other, the elaborated code, had much longer, more formed sentences and could be understood independently of a context. This, so far, is not particularly contentious. The two codes correspond roughly to the formal and informal registers.

Bernstein, however, went further. He claimed that there was different access to these codes depending upon social background. Although Bernstein did not actually state this, the idea grew that whereas middle class children had access to both codes and could use each in appropriate situations, working class children tended only to have access to the restricted code. Because school conducted its business through an elaborated code, these children were handicapped and found it much harder to succeed. The idea of linguistic deprivation or deficit was formed.

Ideas like these led to attempts to improve the success rate of working class children by compensatory education programmes which involved a great deal of attention to language. Some of these programmes tried to teach Standard English to children in ways that paralleled the teaching of foreign languages. The programmes had little measurable success. This was largely because of several misconceptions upon which the programmes were based.

The first problem was the idea that the children were deficient in their linguistic ability. Work by many researchers, notably the American, William Labov, has challenged this view and found that there is no shortage of verbal skill among working class children. The problem is that schools tend neither to provide the right

Children should not be expected to abandon their natural language.

environment in which these children can and will show their skill, nor to value the forms this skill takes. Other researchers have found that children whose language in school consisted almost entirely of one word answers to their teachers' questions had an extremely rich language environment at home. The schools were somehow failing to provide a similarly supportive environment and were thus underestimating the capabilities of their children.

A second problem with language compensation programmes was that they seemed to expect children to abandon the language of their homes in favour of the new forms they were being taught. This was very naive, and ignored the very close link between language and identity. To expect children to abandon their natural language is to expect them to abandon their definitions of what they are. Children, quite naturally, rebel against this.

The overall problem was, and to some extent still is, that schools account for the low success rate of some groups of children by blaming the children themselves, or their homes. Terms such as 'deprived' or 'deficit' imply that the fault is within the children rather than within the school. If, however, all children come to school speaking logically structured and fully formed varieties of language, then the problem is rather that the school fails to recognise this and does not plan its work to take account of it. Some rethinking of the school's role seems necessary.

Celebrating language diversity

Some guidelines for the school's response to language diversity have already emerged from the discussion so far. Three principles can be stated:

1 Schools and teachers should be aware of the varieties of language which their children bring to school with them. This involves listening to the children and discussing things with them, but it may also involve more sustained attempts to forge links with local communities and with parents.

2 Schools need to begin to work with their children as they are, rather than as they would like them to be. This means accepting that children bring a great deal of linguistic expertise to school with them, and planning programmes to make the most of this. It also means attempting to create school and classroom environments in which children can feel confident that their language will be respected and is an appropriate vehicle for learning.

3 Schools should set themselves the goal of increasing the total language awareness of all their children. This means making language itself a much more prominent feature of classroom work.

These principles lead to the idea of schools positively celebrating the language diversity within them, rather than either ignoring it, or seeing it as a problem. Celebrating diversity can have a great many social benefits as children begin to feel that their contributions to school life are important and valued. It can also have many benefits in terms of the development of language competency. Children can be given opportunities to use language in a wider variety of contexts, and also to step back from their use of language to talk about it as an important object in its own right.

There are several possible starting points for this celebration in primary classrooms.

Songs and poems

There is a wealth of recorded folk music which, by its nature, tends to use dialects and accents which may be unfamiliar to children. This can be listened to as part of topic work, dialect expressions can be discussed and children can try to imitate the accents.

Children could be encouraged to find recordings of songs in their own dialects or accents. They could also make their own recordings, perhaps involving parents or grandparents.

Children could collect playground rhymes and compare them with those used in other parts of the country or in other countries.

These suggestions can also profitably be used with children who have other community languages than English. Parents will be the best source of information.

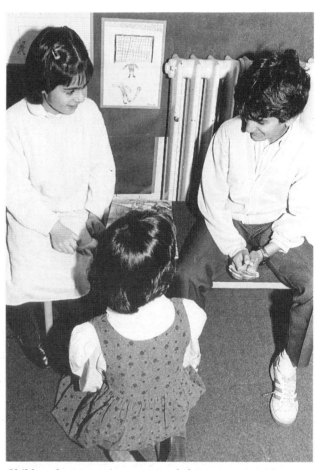

Children love to recite poems and rhymes.

Writing systems

Get the children to make and display collections of alternative writing systems, from Hieroglyphics and Ancient Greek to

Urdu, Russian, Hindi etc. They could collect ways of writing familiar phrases such as 'Good morning' in as many different languages and writing systems as they can. They could examine different writing systems for similarities and find out how modern systems have developed.

Counting systems could also be examined from Roman numerals to modern Arabic numbers (see page 155). Children could learn to count in different languages and dialects. (In the Cumbrian dialect 'one, two, three' becomes 'yan, tyan, tethera'. Several regional versions of this exist.)

Other communications systems could be examined and their uses discussed, for example, Morse Code, Braille, Semaphore, Romany signs etc.

Accents and dialects

Accents and dialects could be discussed directly using recorded examples. Some children will be able to make recordings of their own relations.

They could discuss:

- Why accents and dialects exist,
- Accents and dialects in different countries (children could be asked to listen carefully for accents in TV programmes, for example, Texan accents in *Dallas* and Australian accents in *Neighbours*),
- How to represent accents in writing,
- How accents and dialects are used differently according to situation.

The children could make dialect collections of words for particular things. The plimsolls/pumps/daps collection referred to earlier is a good starting point.

Topic work

Many traditional primary school topics lend themselves to work on language. For example, 'Ourselves', 'Celebrations', 'Communication' all have strong language dimensions. Encourage children to share their experiences of language diversity.

They could begin a collection of newspapers in various languages. These

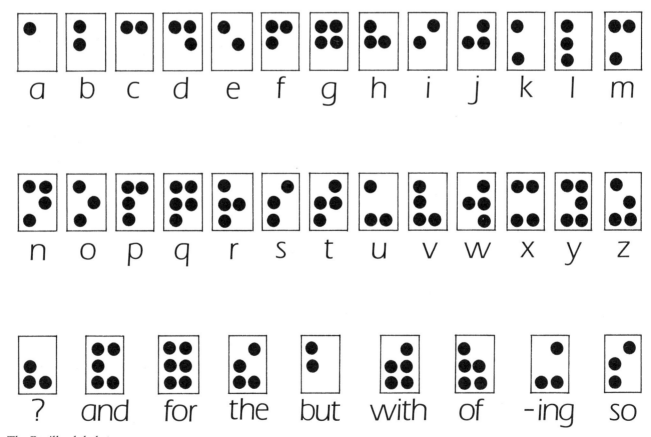

The Braille alphabet

could be examined for similarities in form and content and they could produce their own newspaper to relate their findings.

Plan topics which look directly at aspects of language. For example, 'Language around the world', 'Language in our town', 'Writing', 'The development of English' etc.

Names are a useful focus for language work. Investigate the names of the children in the class. What do they mean and what are their origins?

The most important thing in any work on language diversity is to ensure that children's languages and language varieties are given appropriate respect. The role of the school is to widen children's linguistic competence and appreciation of language. It is not to try to convince them that the way they speak is wrong. The language children bring with them into school is a resource to be built upon and we should never forget that acquiring this language is the greatest learning feat that any child ever accomplishes.

Postscript

For each of the sentences given on page 34 here is a version written in the 'correct' Standard English of 20 years ago, and a brief explanation of the rule which applied. These 'rules' may still be found in modern grammar textbooks.

1 Competitors should try to arrive in good time.
The verb 'try' should always be followed by the preposition 'to'.
2 To whom did you give the book?
There are two rules shown here.
• Sentences should never end with a preposition.
• 'Who' is the form used for a subject, 'whom' for an object. (Nominative/Accusative cases in Latinate grammar descriptions.)
3 Everyone has his weakness.
'Everyone' is a singular form and must take a singular verb.
4 He was better at it than I.
'I' must be used for a subject. The sentence means 'He was better at it than I was.'
5 She did it more quickly than usual.
Verbs must be modified by adverbs. 'Quicker' is a comparative adjective.
6 It is hard even to think of that.
Never split infinitives. This problem has been blamed on the TV series *Star Trek*, with its mission, 'to boldly go where no man has gone before'!
7 This is something with which I cannot deal.
Never end a sentence with a preposition. As Winston Churchill is reputed to have remarked, 'Ending sentences with prepositions is something up with which I cannot put'.

Developing listening
Sarah Tann

Developing listening
Sarah Tann

INTRODUCTION

Concern is frequently voiced about children's ability to listen - or rather their lack of ability. Parents and teachers often say that children just don't seem to listen these days. This assertion acquires the status of fact and is blamed on 'too much television', or 'too much background radio'. Both are assumed to lead to bad habits and encourage children to 'switch off' mentally so that it appears that 'they never listen'.

How justified is this 'common sense' view of children's listening abilities? We need to examine the issue more closely before we can begin to pass judgement. First, what do we mean by 'listen'? The term can be used to refer to a number of aspects: 'pay attention', 'understand or follow', 'remember', 'respond and obey' or 'be able to hear'. These possible meanings each make very different demands upon children, and indicate different types of ability and different possible difficulties.

Secondly, there are different kinds of listening, with different purposes. For example, there is appreciative listening (eg to rhythm, pitch and pattern in both music and poetry); discriminative listening (eg to make fine aural distinctions in phonic sounds when learning a new language or when tackling a new medium of language); reactive listening (eg listening to instructions and acting upon them); and interactive listening (eg in a group, where participants are listening to each other, and perhaps to their own contributions as well).

Thirdly, there are different levels of cognitive demand relating to the ways in which we listen: receptive or fairly passive (sit back and enjoy it); responsive and physically enactive, requiring perhaps some brief information-processing, then getting up and doing something, either immediately or later; and also critical and constructive, requiring participants to interact and participate in order to reorganise and re-state what they understand. Again, each of these makes a different demand on the listener.

Finally, the context and content will demand different things from the listener. Many factors will influence a child's listening, such as who the child is listening to (a familiar or an unfamiliar speaker); what they are listening to (familiar or unfamiliar content); where they are listening (known or unknown setting and situation); why they are being asked to listen (in an essentially passive, physically responsive, or participatory manner).

So what do we really mean when we say that children can't, won't or don't listen? What kinds of listening cause problems, and in what circumstances? We also need to consider to what extent this is due to adults and their inexperience of children's problems as listeners. For example, how effectively do adults let children know what kind of listening is expected? How do we know if children are listening? Are children aware of what they can do to show that they are listening and to indicate whether they understand? How can we help them to understand more clearly the expectations we have for a specific situation?

Before we try to answer such questions, it is important to consider the concept of 'listening' and look at the possible problems posed by the definition of its parameters.

Even if we restrict ourselves to thinking about listening to the spoken word, and thereby ignore listening to environmental or musical sounds, there are still further aspects which need to be clarified. Apart from the distinctions which we have already given, which may each affect children's performance as listeners, there is also the theoretical question of whether and

in what way it is possible to isolate listening from speaking, and indeed, whether one should.

One reason for considering listening separately from speaking may well be that the physical skills involved are different. But if we view listening in its functional context, as part of the communication process, then listening, participating, contributing, talking and speaking evidently have many common features.

As part of the communicative process, when we listen we need to attend, follow, understand, make sense of information and 'make it our own' by adjusting and integrating the new message into our existing understanding. It is both a receptive and a productive process; it requires comprehension and a creative or re-creative response. This may all take place as part of an 'inner dialogue' with or without being put into words. So the cognitive demands made of a listener are similar to those made of a speaker. If the thoughts are put into words, the linguistic demands are similar too. If the listener is in a group, the presence of others also has a social function, regardless of whether or not they make a response.

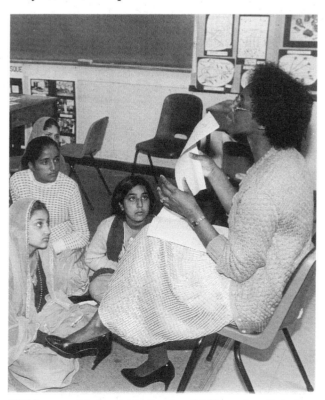

Children need to learn to attend and follow when listening.

43

But if listening is thought of as a separate activity from speaking it can become very passive and non-participatory.

In practical terms, children can become unsure of what they are supposed to do when they are asked to listen. They may be told 'don't talk', or 'don't fidget'. It can soon seem that they mustn't do anything. It could be argued that one of the contributory factors to the notion of a 'listening problem' is that we have tended to separate listening so that it becomes non-participatory, thereby helping to create an impression that listening is passive. This can result in little or no encouragement for children to develop a range of responses which could show that they are listening, and could provide them with a clearer, more active role.

Both listening and speaking, therefore, are active and interactive parts of the communicative process. The more this is emphasised, the less likely listeners are to 'do nothing'.

Furthermore, we need to ask whether it is artificial and unhelpful to separate oracy from literacy. After all, we listen to stories, talk about books and discuss our own writing, as well as using talk to gossip, have discussions, share experiences, ideas and opinions, hold debates, or participate in decision-making and planning sessions. As speakers we need to be aware of listeners' needs in each context, and as listeners we must also be aware of speakers' needs. Feedback for all participants is vital, whether roles are rapidly changing in an interactive situation or are relatively static, as when one person is transmitting information to others. Listening must not be viewed just as part of oracy, but as part of language as a whole.

It is now time to examine the kinds of listening which children experience and to relate this to the kinds of listening which are now being demanded of them within the National Curriculum. We need to consider whether the demands are changing, and how we can help children improve their listening skills.

Interactive listening

Listening and responding to stories, poems and non-fiction

Many children - and teachers - look forward to 'story time'. A great deal of pleasure can be derived from a good story well read. But this isn't always the case! So much depends on the quality of the book, the range of tastes and the concentration span within the group. Much also depends on the quality of the reading. Not all of us read aloud equally well; after all, teachers now have to compete with trained actors and the visual effects on television programmes such as *Jackanory* and *Book Tower*.

We need to distinguish between story-telling and reading a story, for there are considerable differences both for the listener and for the teller or reader. The recent revival in story-telling has encouraged us to realize the potential for audience involvement in the stories, helping to give the listeners an active part.

Story-telling is not just the recitation of a story without using the book. It is a method which breaks down the barrier between reader and listener, enabling teller and listeners to interact and construct a narrative together. It is a weaving together of suggestions. The ideas can be generated by the listeners, but the story is still controlled by the teller, who can select from the ideas offered.

Story-telling allows the teller to invite contributions for a particular purpose, for example to decide the sequence of events, "What could happen next ...?", "Who will ...?", "What might they say ...?", or to make explicit the structure of the narrative "If they did that, then ...", "What could follow ...?", "What would make sense ...?", or to determine behaviour 'in character', "Would they be likely to ...?"

Another way of breaking down the reader-listener barrier is by telling a story rather than reading it. The book then does not come between you and your audience

Children love to take an active part in story-telling.

and prevent eye-contact. Reciting a story without a book can create a more immediate bond between teller and listener because of the greater directness. Suitable stories have to be chosen, rehearsed and presented very carefully, with or without props.

With young children it is important to shorten the time for which we expect them to listen. Many teachers find action rhymes successful for this. These are short and repetitive, allowing the children to react through mime and join in with the choruses. Nursery rhymes and favourite classroom poems can also encourage children to join in. Both the rhyme and the rhythm of poetry encourage children to predict what will come next so that they can participate more confidently, and also develop their appreciative listening by becoming more aware of such aural patterns. Many children enjoy recitation (which is now suggested in the programmes of study at key stage 1, para. 4) whether it is done as a group or individually. It is also a good opportunity for children to learn how to sing their own rhymes and songs in other languages.

Even when reading a story we can find ways to help to make listening more interactive. A way of encouraging children to participate in a story is to make room for them to contribute by, for example, inviting them to name the children in the story or the street where they live. Or the reader can encourage them to create the relevant sound effects when the giant stomps up the stairs or the monster smacks his lips .

Making 'story time' an enjoyable period will encourage children to listen and respond positively to stories and poems (AT 1, Level 1). Another way of encouraging participation is to invite children to guess what will happen next, and why, or to ask, 'How would you have reacted?'. This obviously becomes a more sophisticated activity as the stories grow more complex and the children learn to listen more precisely to the clues in the text or pictures. Talking and listening in groups can encourage children to use inference and deduction to find meanings beyond the literal (AT 2, Level 3).

In addition, children enjoy discussing preferences and can express opinions concerning what has been read (AT 1, Level 2, AT 2, Level 2). This process of analysis and evaluation can begin very early and become a continuing activity which readers adopt throughout their lives in increasingly detailed and satisfying ways.

Listening to each other's stories

Encouraging children to share in each other's story-making provides a chance for children to become the audience for their partner's draft. In this way the partners take on the role of critical listeners to each

Children should be encouraged to read and tell stories to each other.

other. This is a very important role and requires a great deal of sensitivity and tact.

The role of critical listener can take place at the beginning, middle and end of the story-making process. For example, at the very beginning of a 'writers' workshop', children might be asked to spend two minutes thinking what they would like to write about, before spending a further five minutes telling each other about their proposed stories.

At this stage the listener needs to attend carefully to the story outline and then to comment. The listener can also provide support and encouragement, identify ambiguities and possibly suggest places where clarification might be needed. Some classes have developed threefold guidelines such as the following:

• Say two nice things, for example which bits you liked.
• Next ask questions, if you weren't quite clear about parts of it.

• Then make suggestions about how to make the story clearer or better.

Later, when the first draft has been written, dictated or drawn in picture sequence, it can be read to the partner. Again, the listener needs to remember the three steps just outlined.

In addition, the partner rehearsing their story or reading their draft needs to be able to listen to the comments made, understand the reader's perspective, explain their own position and be willing to consider changes. Each partner needs to understand the other in order to be an effective listener.

Articulating such guidelines can help children to appreciate what their role as a listener should be, and to come to know what to listen for and how to respond. It can help them become more effective listeners.

Listening to each other in a discussion group

This form of listening is sometimes considered the most demanding. It requires the participants constantly to switch between being a listener and being a speaker, and also to switch attention between the members of the group. It therefore makes considerable cognitive demands, as well as the social demands involved in handling the group itself, and the linguistic demands of being able to follow what is going on, respond and contribute to an immediate and probably fast-moving conversation.

People sometimes forget the importance of the task itself for a sucessful group discussion. It is necessary to consider whether the task actually needs a group - could it just as successfully be completed by an individual? Also, what resources are needed for the task? Are there physical resources which need to be manipulated and shared and which require collaboration? Or are the children's own imagination and ideas the resources? And what exactly is the problematic aspect of

the task which needs discussion?

Where the cognitive demands of the task vary considerably, group members will vary in their responses. This will affect the talking and listening within the group. The Programmes of Study for English Attainment Target 1, Speaking and Listening, include a long list of contributory skills for interactive group discussions, which include the affective and social skills as well as the cognitive skills needed for a problem-solving task. For example, paragraph 2 touches on the following aspects:

• Developing the attention span.
• Understanding about turn-taking and the timing of contributions.
• Being able to gain and hold the attention of listeners.
• Knowing how to describe experiences, express opinions, articulate feelings.
• Listening to and giving weight to the opinions of others.
• Perceiving the relevance of contributions.
• Adjusting and adapting to views expressed.

Children need to develop their talking and listening skills in groups.

47

• Being able to disagree courteously with an opposing point of view.

One might also add to the last point,
• Being able to ask questions and seek to clarify ambiguities (not just passively accepting and adjusting to others' views).

Attainment Target 1 in science also suggests that children should describe and communicate in small groups (Level 1), ask 'how' and 'why' questions (Level 2), and give an account of an investigation (Level 3). In mathematics children are expected to talk about their own work and ask questions (Level 1), ask and respond (Level 2), explain work being done (Level 3), and present findings orally (Level 4). In all three core subjects, children should be able to argue their case by Level 5. All of these require children to take the role of both listener and speaker.

This is highlighted in the Programmes of Study for English, paragraph 3, and some additional aspects are listed:

• When listening to others, [children are expected] to respond to different ways of talking in different contexts and for different purposes,
• [Children are also expected] to reflect on and evaluate their use of spoken language and to reformulate it to help the listener.

Apart from these general discussion components it is also helpful to consider the different stages through which a discussion may proceed, each of which may benefit from particular skills. In co-operative planning activities, further skills are needed. For example, it is necessary for the group to engage in 'forming' and 'norming' (settling as a group) before 'storming' for ideas and then 'performing'.

For example, a group must define their goals eg is the choice between planning a trip to a farm, a stately home, a nature reserve, or a castle, or is the subject of the planning a school open evening, a local community fun run, lunch-time class clubs etc? They also have to generate alternatives, provide reasons and evidence in order to choose a course of action. Then they must follow through the necessary steps to take and tasks to share in order to achieve their goal.

In each of these steps, the participants must listen to each contribution and to the overall progress of the discussion in order to make effective contributions. Clearly it is difficult to achieve this sort of simultaneous contributing and monitoring. Built-in steps for review can be introduced so that the group learns to remember to undertake reviews regularly during the course of the

In group discussions it is important to listen carefully to each contribution.

discussion to ensure that the discussion stays on track. Furthermore, if some kind of record of the brainstorming is drawn up, there will be a verifiable pool of contributions which can be referred to, which will be more reliable than the participants' memories of what was said and when. Such records are useful in discussions, as they relieve the listener from having to remember past contributions as

well as attending to present ones.

In order to achieve this level of contribution the listener can be helped to become aware of all the contributory features of group discussion so that they know what to listen for and how to make positive contributions which will help to lead the discussion to a successful conclusion.

Reactive listening

Critical listening to an extended narrative or exposition

Learning to listen to a long speech can be a demanding activity. In AT 1, Level 2, children should be able to describe an event, and at Level 3 they should be able to relate real or imaginary events in a connected narrative.

What does the speaker need to be aware of in terms of the listener's needs? The level of demand differs with the differing activities. For example, young

children are often expected to listen to each other's 'news' at the beginning of the day. This is often very personal, not involving other people, and it is possibly not of interest to anyone else. However, teachers expect children to listen and attend. We need to ask ourselves why we ask children to perform in this way and what the speaker or listener learns from it. Perhaps the speaker feels valued - by the teacher at least - and can gain confidence through speaking in such a public forum. But do the children also get better at speaking? There are a number of different features of this sort of speech - for example, speaking up and delivering information, structuring and sequencing information, anticipating the listener's needs and making the meaning clear.

We also need to ask what the listener's role is. Is it to attend to the speaker, valuing what they have to say? Is it to show interest non-verbally by looking attentive as well as listening, or verbally by becoming an active participant?

As already mentioned, both the speaker and whoever is leading the session can help the listener, and invite him or her to play a more active part. Such participant strategies frequently adopted by teachers include inviting named others to compare the 'news' they have just heard with something similar which they have done recently, or to invite suggestions of what they might have done or felt in the same situation. Teachers can also encourage the listeners to ask questions for further clarification, so the speaker can provide more detail, or an explanation of why or how the event happened, and what happened next, as well as indicating their personal reaction and feelings. Using these key ideas (or similar ones) can help both speakers and listeners become more aware of the listener's needs when following an extended narrative, and therefore what the speaker should offer. Indeed, by English AT 1, Level 3, children are expected to be able to 'listen with an increased span of concentration to other children and adults, asking and responding to questions and commenting on what has been said.'

The ability to listen and take in information aurally is often assessed in 'answer sessions' conducted by the teacher. Much research has already identified the issues associated with different questioning strategies, but we also need to remember the impact of the 'response time' allowed, ie the time allowed for the listener to take in the question, select information and reorganize it to formulate an answer. On average teachers allow two seconds before they repeat, rephrase or redirect the question. This would seems an unreasonable strain on the listener!

As well as telling their 'news', children also present talks or report back on the progress of projects and the processes involved. This type of talking may also involve extended oral narrative presentations (see Maths and Science Level 3). These may make additional particular demands on their listeners, who may subsequently be expected to play a more critical and constructive role as response partners.

Again, it is important for the listeners to know what their role is, eg to ask questions, or to take notes for a specific purpose. It will help if they already have some familiarity with the content of the talk, perhaps because this has been discussed previously at a draft stage, or because it is part of a class project in which everyone is involved. Otherwise the listener needs to be prepared by being given a brief overview before the speaker launches into the detail. Also, the information needs to be 'chunked' and 'labelled' through the use of sub-headings and sections. These signal to the listener when there is a change and indicate what subsequent information will be about.

Awareness of these structures can provide listeners with a framework to use in developing the note-taking skills which they may well need after transition to the secondary stage of education.

Listening to take notes is a particular form of reactive listening. Although not a common demand for primary age children, it can be a very useful skill to begin to acquire. For example, on school trips or when a visitor comes to the school for the children to interview as part of their investigatory work, the children may need to listen carefully and to extract information. It is important to prepare the listeners by deciding what information they want, how to note it, and what to do with it. Children may even have formulated a questionnaire of items to ask a speaker. Even with this degree of preparation, children may still find it difficult to take in the information unless it comes exactly as they anticipate it. So if in answering one question the speaker goes on to develop a related point, the children may not recognise that this in fact answers a subsequent question; instead they will ask the subsequent question and expect a further answer.

Making notes, jotting down key words or phrases to remind one of of things just heard or read, is in fact a very demanding activity. Brief phrases may not involve too much of the physical labour of writing, but children will also require an ability to analyse, select and summarise. They may often find it easier to represent the information by a labelled diagram or annotated picture which allows them to undertake the cognitive demands and to form images for selected aspects, before they have to try to put their understanding into words.

Listening to brief information and instructions

The ability to follow and give simple instructions is given prominence in English AT 1, beginning in Level 1. By Level 3, instructions and messages are likely to come not only from the teacher in person, but also via a telephone. This kind of listening is for a shorter period, but it is more intense in that the exact wording must be remembered, rather than just the gist of the contents.

This sort of listening can involve remembering and learning, retelling, reciting, and passing information on to others. Such skills are the basis of many games such as Chinese Whispers, Simon Says, Pass the Portrait (where child A describes a person to child B who tells child C who draws it for child A ...) and frequently feature in published materials such as *Listen, Think, Do*.

The adult (for it is usually an adult giving the instructions) can help the listener in ways like those already outlined. The listener should be alerted to the need to listen, and the fact that this information is relevant and important to them. Then the listener needs to know generally what it is going to be about, what they have to do, when they are supposed to respond and what happens next.

Apart from preparing the listener in this way, the speaker can also encourage the listener to participate in constructing and giving the instructions. Many instructions in class are routine, or can be deduced from the situation. Children can therefore be invited to think for themselves and for each other and suggest what the instructions should be, instead of relying entirely on the teacher for this. The teacher can invite the children to explain and remind each other, or to decide collectively and thus encourage independence and interdependence. This takes up more time, of course, and is not for emergency situations, but it can turn teacher-given routines into a learning activity for the children.

The game 'Simon says' involves specific listening skills.

Discriminative listening for fine aural distinctions

Listening and reading

In order for children to develop into readers who can read with expression (AT 2, Level 3) they need to listen to other readers, and also to themselves, perhaps at first on tape. Attention to the meaning conveyed through intonation, for example, will also help with punctuation. Punctuation is the written form of intonation, and helps not only to convey information through the word order of phrases and sentences, but often to add to the information carried by particular words through varying the stress.

Children can be encouraged to develop close attentiveness to word meanings through listening to readings. Useful examples might be the giant's form of language in Roald Dahl's *The B.F.G.* and the 'miscues' in Michael Rosen's *Hairy Tales and*

Nursery Crimes. This is an aural equivalent of 'scanning' in reading!

Listening for aesthetic awareness

Fine aural discrimination is also important in encouraging a more creative and aesthetic awareness of language. For example, in the programmes of study (AT 3) teachers are encouraged to invite children to play with words, to become more aware of rhyme, rhythm and pattern, and to write jingles, poems and riddles. All this presupposes that children have an ear for language and have had experience in listening to the music in words.

An activity which children often enjoy is a musical version of taking the register, where either the teacher sings 'good morning' to each child using a different rhythm or melodic shape which the child has to imitate, or the child sings 'good morning' and the teacher has to imitate. It may take longer but the children certainly listen! There is much published material which can help encourage fine aural discrimination, particularly tapes of environmental noises to be identified: if these are classified by the children as well it can become a more creative and demanding activity.

Listening and looking for patterns

Any word-play can also help encourage an awareness of spelling patterns, which might be aural or visual. In AT 4, Level 1, children need to know letter shapes, speech sounds and letter names, and in AT 4, level 2, they should know that spelling has patterns.

After USSR, ERIC or another silent reading activity children can be encouraged to pick out any new, unusual, sonorous, or problematic words to share with the rest of the class. This may generate a discussion about other words which rhyme with the word under discussion, or which sound like it but are spelt differently (generating a discussion of alternative ways of spelling the same 'sound patterns'). Chosen words may suggest others with a similar prefix or suffix, or a similar root, or associated meanings.

Whole passages may be chosen for a variety of reasons, such as humour, pathos or vividness. This can encourage children to read their books with attention to the aesthetic and effective impact and to consider how the writer achieves this.

In sharing such discoveries, children listen closely to the sound and impact of the words as well as to the subsequent discussion - which reinforces the essential integration of listening with reading and writing as well as speaking and responding.

Listening to tapes of songs and rhythms helps to encourage fine aural discrimination.

Monitoring listening

As with all other aspects of classroom learning, close monitoring is valuable in so far as it provides us with systematically collected information about children's competencies which then can enable us to make sure that the individual's needs are met and their learning environment enhanced. The purpose of monitoring is to improve teaching and learning. If it becomes so burdensome that it inhibits either then it becomes pointless.

What to monitor: teaching provision and learning progress

We have outlined many different variables which could form the basis for distinguishing the different kinds of listening demands made upon a child. These could be used to monitor the provision in our own classrooms so that we can assess whether the opportunities we provide are suitably varied to cover the full range of situations and to enable children to demonstrate what they can do.

We can use the same set of variables to monitor each child's level of performance, for the National Curriculum requires us to keep 'teacher records' to show how schemes of work have been implemented in the classroom, as well as 'pupil records' to monitor individual progress.

To make such a monitoring exercise feasible rather than overwhelming we need to become familiar with the Attainment Targets and with each Statement of Attainment. Most Statements of Attainment are multiple statements which include at least two sub-components. English alone, therefore, probably generates 150 criteria we could be monitoring! From this bank, we need to select only those which will be most useful in informing classroom practice, or about which we may be concerned in relation to particular children, and which will contribute to the information which we need to collect in order to fulfil the requirements of the reporting procedures at Key Stages 1 and 2.

It will not be necessary to monitor all the attributes for each child, particularly as (to date) it is probable that we will only be required to report in terms of the three Profile Components (speaking and listening, reading, writing). However, on a day-to-day basis we need information in greater detail, so that we can organise and manage activities each day. In addition, we will need enough information to feel sure that across the whole school (and between schools) there is sufficient awareness of what each child has experienced and achieved, so that continuity and progression will prevail.

The Statutory Orders for English at Key

It is very important that teachers keep accurate records to monitor progress.

Stage 1 expect that pupils should be able to listen in the following ways:

● Respond to simple instructions ('reactive');
● Listen attentively and respond to stories ('interactive');
● Use phonic (and other) clues in reading ('discriminative').

The programmes of study also expect that children will retell stories, recite poems, and play with language - making up jingles, rhymes and word games involving spelling patterns. Such activities will entail both discriminative and aesthetic forms of listening.

It is important to clarify what a Statement of Attainment might mean in the context of a real classroom. For example, it would be possible to list what you would expect to see or hear from the child as evidence of what counts as achieving that attribute. This list of 'indices' generated from a selection of Statements of Attainment could form the basis of an observation schedule which a teacher could use to focus monitoring during classroom activities, if they were particularly concerned about an individual's attainment in a particular area. If Statements of Attainment are clarified as a whole school, there will be greater consistency in interpreting what we mean when we say a child is 'at' a particular level.

How to monitor: recording methods and managing time

The NCC pack includes broadsheets on record keeping and assessment, and Primary English 1 and 2. These suggest observation and monitoring but offer little advice except to use The Primary Language Record devised by ILEA. This suggests a twofold approach. First, in the Autumn and Summer terms, the teacher summarises a conference with the child's parents about their perceptions and concerns relating to their child's language development. In the Spring term, the teacher makes a record of his or her own observation of the child as a language user. Secondly, about once a month, a set of 'observation/diary sheets' are filled in; these record a sample of a child's oral experiences and competencies. The observation sheets allow the teacher to note the tasks undertaken, and also their social context, in a matrix form. They also give space for open-ended comments on and quotation of the child's use of language. A given framework for comments suggests 'conversation moves' (initiating, responding), 'social moves' (taking turns, encouraging others), 'logical moves' (categorising, evaluating), 'metalinguistic moves' (monitoring one's own strategies). It is evident that this framework covers the speaking part of the profile component more fully than the listening part.

Now that the National Curriculum has provided us with a more detailed set of categories in the Statements of Attainment it would seem useful to employ them. The open-ended diary format may be suitable for some teachers, though it may be slower and more cumbersome, as well as being difficult to fill in during a teaching session. An A4-size schedule of selected Statements of Attainments and their indices - to be used with particular children on a specific occasion to help to focus attention on an aspect about which we are not sure - may be much quicker and more manageable, though no schedule is adequate and one would need at least half a side of A4 with room to add brief comments and quotes! Such a semi-structured 'running record' could be helpful sometimes in sharpening our observations and helping us to focus on specifics so as to inform planning and provision and increase awareness of a child's progress.

Time will be at a premium, so ways of finding the most effective use of time will be crucial. It is important to invest time, before a session, in analysing what learning we anticipate the likely activities will promote, and in selecting which children we will focus attention on for brief periods of

Teachers keep abreast of the National Curriculum Statements of Attainment.

observation. This will enable us to use our time with greater efficiency, as we will have decided what targets, which children, and when to watch. Just as we successfully train children not to interrupt us when we are reading or conferring with a child, so we can train them not to interrupt if we are monitoring for, say, periods of just two or even five minutes.

Teachers already monitor constantly, using the eyes at the back of their heads! Teachers keep enormous quantities of information about their children in their heads. We need to realise that reserving time to observe and monitor is not something to feel guilty about because you are not 'teaching'. Systematic monitoring by regularly sampling children's learning behaviour will inform our teaching and increase our ability to enhance the learning opportunities for the children we want to support.

It is not so much a question of needing to learn a whole new set of skills; we must rather make explicit that which we already know and do, so that we can share it with the children, their parents and our other colleagues. Task analysis, rigorous observation of children as they learn and systematic reflection upon the listeners and speakers in our classrooms could help to improve the education we offer our children.

Structuring contexts for exploratory talk Terry Phillips

INTRODUCTION

If, heaven forbid, talk were ever to be the subject of a productivity audit, it would emerge as good value for money. It would be rated 'highly cost-effective' because it allows us to do more than one job at a time - it is multi-functional. It enables us to shape information and ideas as we talk about them. It can also be used to exchange attitudinal messages at the same time as communicating basic information. In other words we do not simply transmit and receive information and ideas when we talk to each other but interpret them and develop attitudes, values, and feelings about them. It is true, of course, that all speech takes place in a wider social and political context and that consequently speakers' ideas and values are influenced by the times in which they live, but it is in each individual interaction that they are explored and developed. Let us look briefly at how this happens.

In the act of telling someone else about something a speaker makes choices. She selects particular words and automatically excludes others. For example, if she chooses to call her young cat 'cuddly little thing' she has chosen at the same time not to call it 'naughty kitten'. She also chooses the order in which she will present her information, often placing the most important piece at the beginning or at the very end where it is most likely to be noticed - 'that kitten...we took it to my nannie's but it was ever so naughty'. She chooses, too, to juxtapose bits of information in ways that create new meanings, as in 'my bike's got a flat tyre...Peter had it last', which implies, but does not state, that Peter damaged the bike. By making these kinds of linguistic choices speakers shape their information; no speaker ever delivers information unmediated, it has always been actively - if unknowingly - constructed. The listener, of course, has to interpret this constructed information and in turn make her own choices in the light of that.

Every speaker makes intuitive judgements about the 'worth' of what other people are saying. For instance, she subconsciously 'reads' their intonation and non-verbal signals, so that if someone grins whilst speaking she treats their information as potentially funny, and if they use a rising tone at the end of an utterance she hears it as questioning. In doing this she implicitly acknowledges that information is not to be heard in a neutral way but as having a 'value'. It is impossible to separate the communication of attitudes from the communication of information; there are a range of ways, apart from the two already mentioned, in which our spoken language is equipped to keep the two together. If speakers emphasise a specific piece of information by stressing it we know without thinking that it should be treated as important. If they hedge a statement with 'if', 'but', or 'maybe' we understand at the same intuitive level that they are uncertain about it. Similarly, if they assert their information using 'must', 'should', and 'will' (what linguists call modalities), or state it baldly, in an unmodified form (eg 'all rivers flow to the sea'), we realise that they believe strongly in what they say and want us to believe it too. All these linguistic devices allow a speaker to communicate her attitudes and feelings without needing to spell them out explicitly, and enable her listeners to monitor them without having to speak about them directly. It follows that every verbal exchange of factual

A speaker selects particular words and the order in which she tells something.

information is also willy-nilly a subconscious exploration of implicit views, attitudes, and values.

From time to time the process of exploration moves from the subconscious and implicit to the conscious and explicit. This shift happens when we use talk to summarise or comment upon each other's suggestions. It also occurs when we speculate by taking half-formulated or 'immature' ideas and sharpening them up in discussion. It happens again when we discuss how the conversation itself is 'going', ask whether the language is appropriate, and discuss things like turns and interruptions. When speakers use forms of exploratory talk which involve them in explicit consideration of what lies behind information and ideas, they develop their *meta-cognitive competence* - their ability to organise ideas about ideas. When they explore the conversation itself they develop their *meta-linguistic competence* - their ability to handle talk about talk. Experience of these seems to contribute to the ability to plan, execute, and reflect upon complex activities.

All talk, then, is exploratory in so far as it is always used to construct information and fathom its value, but some forms of talk are intentionally so. To take account of this in our classrooms we must organise the teaching and learning of ideas in ways that ensure children have the necessary time to explore information, that give proper status to the exploration of ideas, attitudes and values, and that encourage critical reflection.

Intuitive exploration

Making sense of new information

Teachers can often intervene positively to provide learning contexts that favour exploratory talk, whether it is the intuitive kind or the more deliberate forms that have been outlined. At the intuitive end teachers can begin by offering regular discussion time for children to familiarise themselves with new information. Many schools already set aside a considerable amount of time for introducing new information; the National Curriculum insists that they should *all* do so. Children need to be helped to come to terms with these official bodies of knowledge. Psychology and our own experience tell us that every time a child learns something new she has to adjust her view of how things are, and 'accommodate' the new items in her 'world-picture'. Unless she does this the facts remain nothing more than inert collectable items. In this sense, unassimilated facts are like the free gifts sometimes found in cereal packets, they are enticing for a moment or two while they have novelty value but are then discarded and forgotten because they have no real purpose. The process of assimilation is often initially a slow one, but it can be made easier if a child has the opportunity to explore new ideas in discussion. If she is allowed time to talk about it, she can 'try out' newly-acquired information over which she has only hesitant command, learn from other people's responses, and 'stabilise' the information on the basis of true understanding. Despite the fact that time seems to be in short supply in today's primary school, it is essential that a little of it is given over to providing a breathing space for children to come to terms with new information. Time spent at an early juncture will actually be time saved because the better understanding which a child gains at that stage will enable her to move more rapidly through subsequent activities that depend on familiarity with official bodies of knowledge.

Some children can make sense of new information in their heads, without externalising it through talk, but most learn more readily through having the opportunity to 'chew it over' in discussion. There are a range of ways in which this basic kind of exploratory talk can be built in to a school day. When a child first learns about 'fractions' in a maths lesson, for instance, ten minutes can be allocated for discussion about all the things which she associates with the word. In the same way, if she has learnt that Newcommen and Watt invented the first steam engines, she can be given a short while to explore her notion of 'engines', which she is almost certain to understand to be something different from the Newcommen-Watt ones. On another occasion, if, in preparation for a visit to the local newspaper office, a class has collected information on 'printing' by studying reference books and other resource materials, small groups can compare the information they have culled and explore any differences individuals might have discovered in what their sources claim. To make the necessary arrangements for simple exploratory discussions to be planned into programmes of learning, teachers have to anticipate the point where a need is most likely to occur.

Solving problems

To help children come to terms with new information, teachers need only create space for the process of assimilation to happen. To *guarantee* that exploratory talk serves its intended purpose, however, the 'chewing over' stage needs to be followed by another in which children have to apply the

new information to the solution of a problem. Talk is context dependent, so when a child's language reflects a loss of interest in what she is doing it makes no sense to complain about the 'poor quality of the talk' when what is necessary is a change in the context. Such a change can be made by introducing a problem-solving activity after a familiarisation one. Ideally the problem should as naturally as possible out of on-going work - ie it should be a *real* problem

A visit to a newspaper office can encourage a range of exploratory talk.

which the teacher, from her knowledge of the field and of the children, has anticipated. This will increase the chance that exploratory talk will lead to a practical outcome. However, although a well-prepared teacher can predict some of the real problems which will emerge at particular moments during an activity, it would be difficult for anyone to structure learning so that all problem-solving arises naturally. So if classrooms are to have a problem-solving orientation, and children are to come to regard exploratory talk about information as an automatic precursor to exploring it further in practical contexts, then it will be necessary to devise *realistic* problems instead, ie problems which the teacher 'engineers' by providing materials or situations into which a dilemma is structured, but which she makes sure are related to the children's current concerns.

Becoming more aware

Exploring by arguing and reasoning

Talk can, of course, be used to explore thinking in a more deliberate way than happens in brief 'chewing over' discussions; for example, when a child sets out to 'argue a case' or 'explain' (ie give reasons for) 'a course of action'. There are many ways other than through reasoned argument that a child can indicate the extent of her understanding, of course. When she successfully 'follows instructions related to a task', a child demonstrates her comprehension of them without using spoken language at all. When she 'describes a recent event', she shows that she has imposed some sort of logic on it. When she 'gives an accurate and detailed account' of what she has recently seen or taken part in, she reveals an awareness of that logic. But schools (together with law-courts) are peculiar in valuing ability to make understanding explicit in talk, through the language of logic and deduction.

Reasoned argument not only provides evidence for others of the child's thinking, as suggested by the National Curriculum, but also allows her to clarify it to herself.

Teachers can create 'argumentative classrooms' where there are plenty of genuine reasons for children to persuade each other. An 'argumentative classroom' is one where teachers and children alike are willing to explore publicly what they are thinking and to ask everyone else to do the same. An 'argumentative classroom' is also a place where children have developed an expectation that their point of view is valued, and their challenges to other points of view welcomed. Time spent by a child on activities which oblige her to persuade and justify will also be time spent exploring her own thinking.

An exploratory approach to learning is a habit which a child acquires through experience, and provided that she has had sufficient experience she will readily handle the argumentative talk which is characteristic of that approach. A child's ability to argue and reason successfully depends less on her age, than upon the way her teacher has shaped the class's expectations by building 'argumentative moments' into the school day. If she is in a class where teacher and children often explore ideas together, and children regularly work together in groups to resolve issues, a five-year-old can explore an issue of importance to her as effectively as an eleven-year-old, though the topics she will find interesting are likely to be different.

An 'argumentative moment' can occur when a six-year-old has covered herself with paint and the teacher arranges for the whole class to explore ways of keeping their clothes clean. Or it could happen when a group of ten-year-olds, having heard about the underpaid nineteenth century factory worker forced to steal food to feed a large family, are invited by their teacher to explore the moral dilemma involved. The teacher of a class of seven-year-olds, having seen children squabbling about observance of a rule during a game, can create an 'argumentative moment' by getting the children to explain to her how their game is played and whether any rules could be changed to make it easier. On each occasion the teacher's intervention will create a context in which the children become actively involved in discussing the issue to unearth its implicit values. No child will have been asked to take part in a discussion which has been artificially set up for the primary purpose of practising explanantion and and justification. Each discussion will have arisen within a context in which it makes sense.

A curriculum which succeeds in ensuring that children use their language for specific purposes within the context of on-going learning requires careful long-term planning, and the development of

An ideal 'argumentative moment' can occur in painting when the whole class can explore ways of keeping their clothes clean.

exploratory modes of thinking only becomes second nature where a regular demand for exploration and challenge has been created.

The language of argument and reasoning

It should be self-evident that a teacher's main role in seeking to develop exploratory talk in the classroom is to see that children have a wide range of opportunities to use it for exploratory purposes. In language, there is no one-to-one relationship between function and form, so although children might be able to hone their discussion skills by reflecting on the way they use talk in particular situations, they are most unlikely to benefit from examining something like the 'quality' of the causal connectives ('don't you think it would have been better to begin with "because?"'). Teachers themselves do need to know what to look out for, though, if only to avoid being trapped into seeing certain forms as inadequate and not up to the job.

It is essential to understand that primary school children rarely explain and justify themselves in the way that professional advocates do. It is more likely that evidence of a child's comprehension will come from the manner in which she fits information together - the way that she sequences it and gives it cohesion - rather than the extent to which she is explicit about causes and effects. When she does actually use them, her most common causal connectives will almost certainly be 'cos', 'so','if' and 'though'. Words like 'consequently' and 'therefore' will not be within her range. It would be foolish to attempt to encourage a primary age child to talk like a lawyer or a judge and to explain and justify as a professional would. It makes sense to encourage children to explore through argumentative discussion using their own appropriate language.

Exploring experience through anecdote

Propositions and values are also evaluated through anecdote. Narratives, including anecdotes, are the primary means by which we shape and organise our experience. It is less often recognised that they are also vehicles for evaluating experiences and drawing lessons from life. Anecdotes are often introduced into classroom conversations to illustrate a specific point or to summarise a general point; indeed many anecdotes have a coda which makes a specific value judgement (eg '...perhaps that was the reason my nanny lost her purse'). There are many ways in which, as teachers, we can encourage children to engage in this further form of exploratory talk. They could be asked to discuss an incident in a story, for instance. A group of children invited to respond to the drowning of the heroine in Katherine Paterson's *Bridge to Terabithia* are almost certain to swap anecdotes about their own experiences of the river, of

Telling anecdotes are the primary means by which we shape and organise our experiences.

friendship, and of great loss. As they do so they will explore their feelings and shape their values in relation to a matter of considerable human significance. Teachers can share suitable personal experiences with their classes too. A group of girls, in response to a personal story from their teacher about the clothes she wore as a pupil, will tell each other anecdotes about their mothers wearing fashion clothes to work but not letting them wear similarly stylish clothes to school; in this way they are exploring the concept of 'double standards'. They may never employ the language of causality or justification outlined earlier, but they are nevertheless reasoning and sorting things out for themselves. Anecdotal talk is often regarded pejoratively, as something which is harmless but of very little educational value. This is a misconception of what anecdote does: it not only facilitates the exploration of experience, but also enables the non-logical exploration of values.

Achieving reflexivity

Exploring values through 'critical discourse'

Narrative is perhaps the most natural way for children to explore values because it allows them to do it incidentally in the course of exploring their experiences. There is, however, another mode of exploratory talk that encourages reflection upon values in a more deliberately critical manner. Speakers use this mode of talk, which will be called here 'critical discourse', to comment upon relevance and upon the distinction between fact and opinion. It is also used to make explicit evaluations of the truth of what has been said. It is the kind of talk which most primary school teachers would think of as more suitable for secondary age pupils, and certainly at its most formal it is entirely inappropriate for the young and critically inexperienced. There are some less formal versions of 'critical discourse', however, which are accessible to certain argumentatively-oriented children, usually in the latter part of their primary school career. If, and only if, children have had plenty of opportunity to engage in most of the forms of exploratory talk discussed so far in this chapter, and if they have developed an openess to supportive critical advice from their peers, then they are ready to be asked to explore things through critical discussion.

Readiness for critical discourse does not necessarily mean ability to explore critically from a generalised - or public - position, however. Movement towards the de-centring that makes critical discourse possible occurs in stages. Long before children are able to consider things from the point of view of an abstract, unidentifiable public, they are capable of taking (imaginatively, at least) the perspective of another specific individual. The teacher's role is to create relatively informal and realistic contexts in which the views and concerns of specific others can be explored. Speakers, like writers, always have to consider how to present their message to the audience they are addressing, but they are rarely obliged to consider the message itself from a perspective other than their own. As a culmination of extensive experience of exploring things from their own position, children can be encouraged to de-centre and look at it from someone else's.

There is a small set of activities which would encourage primary age children to listen critically and to respond in a similar manner. Teachers can and do set aside time specifically for discussing local news. If the local newspaper had carried a report of a trader being fined for Sunday opening, the children might be invited to discuss the case for and against Sunday trading from the perspective of a do-it-yourself enthusiast (who might be based on a person they know), and from the perspective of a shop employee. Or if housing developments are occurring in the neighbourhood, the children could be asked to explore the effect

Children will gain a truer understanding of the issues involved in Sunday opening if they interview traders.

the development might have upon traffic density in the older-established streets, and to do it from the perspective of a young person living on the new estate, and an elderly resident in the affected vicinity. These activities satisfy the criterion of realistic context, and ensure that at least two points of view are explored. Children could be critical of the people representing the contrary view to their own, and strengthen their case by distinguishing fact from opinion etc. As always, however, real contexts are preferable to artificial ones, so the children would probably gain a truer understanding of the issues involved if they were to interview real protagonists rather than attempt to project themselves into other people's minds. If a realistic (rather than a real) context is created, it must be handled convincingly. A decontextualised task may produce a form of exploratory talk, but it will not promote an exploratory approach to learning.

Speculating and hypothesising

There is one more form of exploratory talk still to consider, and that is the talk which speakers use to ask 'what if...' and 'suppose ...'. In the primary school it would be unusual to have a discussion *exclusively* for the purpose of putting and testing formal hypotheses; most discussion of the 'what if ...' kind is more loosely speculative than this, and usually occurs in the context of a wider rational argument or reflection on experience. When talk does turn to speculating and informed hypothesising, though, it often changes the nature of the conversation significantly, particularly if the children concerned live in an 'argumentative classroom'.

Characteristically, speculative discussion will have long episodes when the same 'hypothesis' remains 'in play', and speakers will keep returning to suggestions which have been neither rejected outright nor wholeheartedly accepted. To keep their options open as long as possible children often prevent closure with 'yes but...' arguments. There is no urgent need for agreement, and consequently no loss of face

for anyone if agreement is not reached. Speculation is a form of exploratory talk in the same tradition as 'trying out' information to see if it fits the personal world-picture, and thinking about 'what might have been' in the course of telling an anecdote. It can be a valuable means of contemplating alternatives, even indeed of allowing the possibility of the co-existence of more than one alternative at a time. Teachers who have brought their class up in the tradition can expect speculative exploration to arise often and spontaneously during the course of all sorts of discussions.

A good message can usually bear repeating, so as a way of reiterating the point that there is usually more than one alternative, we can plan 'What about if...' workshops. Although these would take place in specially designated time, they would be related to a bigger activity, and would ask a question to which 'what about if...' responses were invited. Relevant speculative discussion is likely to be prompted by one of three types of circumstance. Firstly, where there is a need to assemble a collection of ideas before moving to the next part of an activity. Children could get together in groups to

Speculative discussion is a valuable means of contemplating alternatives.

brainstorm a range of alternative solutions to the sort of question typified by, 'How might we go about enlisting the help of national musical personalities in our drive to get a fully equipped school orchestra?', before devising an action plan and putting it into operation. Secondly, where there is an interest in imagining what it would be like to do something which no human has done. Children might first discuss and then dramatise or paint the ideas they have in response to a question like 'How do you think it would feel if you could fly under your own power?'. Finally, where there is some educational value in doing so, it could be initiated by taking something which is hypothetical at the point of discussion but which can be tested subsequently. The questions 'How might we solve the litter problem in the school environment?' and 'What reduces friction?' are both in this category. Because this third type of question is intended to generate a more traditional form of hypothesis which is open to 'scientific' testing, it is likely to move speakers closer to reasoned argument than towards imaginative play with the idea. Testable hypothesising is to that extent less exploratory than other forms of speculation.

Setting the ground rules

Ground rules will need to be established to promote exploratory talk as a natural mode of classroom discourse. Teachers play a key part in setting these rules; indeed, a study by Mary Willes (1981) has shown how children are taught them from their very first term in school. However, the few rules which most teachers insist on for class discussion, rules such as 'no calling out', 'don't talk whilst someone else is', 'speak clearly' etc, are often invoked but rarely discussed. And, like many classroom rules, they refer to procedures which must be followed but do not provide reasons why or expose principles. As work by Edwards and Mercer (1987) has demonstrated, the quality of learning and the nature of classroom interaction are enhanced when teachers formulate *explicit ground rules*

'Solving the litter problem in school' is an issue that is likely to give rise to a reasoned argument.

that focus on processes and principles.

In whole class discussion the teacher is an authority figure whether she likes it or not because she controls both the turn-taking and the agenda. For this reason, whole-class discussion is often thought to be a context in which satisfactory exploratory talk is unlikely to develop. If, however, it is used firstly as a context to establish ground rules and secondly to encourage examination of the principles which underpin them, then class discussion can play a significant part in the development of exploratory talk. For instance, in a teacher-led lesson a procedural rule which stated:

• no child will dismiss another child's contribution if the contribution is seriously intended

could become the subject of discussion to

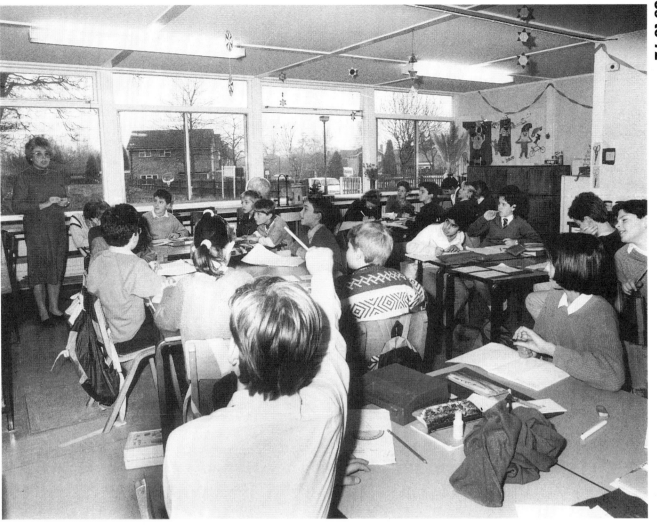

It is important that ground rules are established for classroom discussion.

expose the principle that:

• all speakers deserve to have the strengths and weaknesses of their statements given equal consideration because we gain confidence from knowing our strengths and we learn from our weaknesses.

Class discussion can also be used to give the children responsibility, in negotiation with their teacher, for actually setting some of the rules. If a child is invited to share in the precise formulation of ground rules and the principles behind them, her sense of herself as active decision-maker is bound to be enhanced.

Although small group discussion is obviously more congenial to exploratory talk, both because it allows each person more turns and because it can have a more flexible agenda, ironically it is a slightly more difficult context in which to establish the ground rules. Apart from the fact that teachers are often excluded from small group discussion, which makes it difficult to influence what happens, the rules themselves need to be much more flexible than for class discussion. Confidence, audibility, explicitness, attentive listening, and the ability to take a turn without interrupting, are all valuable attributes for any speaker to possess. But different kinds of talk are appropriate for different purposes, and small group exploratory talk can often be effective when it is full of hesitations, changes of direction, overlaps, and interruptions. All these things occur naturally when a speaker is working tentatively towards new ideas, or becoming excited and committed to them. The most helpful thing teachers can do to promote effective exploratory talk in small groups is to see that the ground rules reflect these

71

features. If a teacher proposes that questions should never be answered without some sort of discussion, and that groups should always attempt to list 'things for further exploration' at the end of a discussion, she will be indicating that rapid closure and group consensus are not always the norm, and that the arguing out of ideas is more important than reaching total, and sometimes superficial, agreement. Perhaps the most important ground rule of all though would be:

• all speakers are expected to examine ideas, challenge assumptions, and speculate about alternatives.

• that ground rule captures the essence of a classroom where exploratory talk has a high priority and the contexts have been structured to promote 'argumentative discourse'.

FOOTNOTE: the extent of a child's experience of a range of forms of exploratory talk is to some extent related to the child's age: she is more likely to have a greater amount of experience the older she is. Given that she has that experience, however, there appear to be no cognitive constraints on her ability to explore critically.

Talk in the early years
Margaret Armitage

Talk in the early years
Margaret Armitage

INTRODUCTION

What is meant by 'talking to learn in the early years'? Is it any different from the normally happy chatter of a group of young children as they sit around a table engaged in a variety of activities? Is the talk helping them to organise and make sense of the task? The answer is obviously 'yes', provided the talk is focused on the task. A child's talk is often of a descriptive or narrative type. It is fictional and directive. She learns about language through using it. But 'talking to learn' is at a deeper level than everyday language. It involves the child in:

- 'Hearing what I think, so I know what I mean'.
- Searching for means of expression which give important information to the 'audience'.
- Attempting to describe a point of view, or thoughts, feelings and ideas which really matter to her and to the audience.
- Verbalising not just the 'what', but the 'how' and the 'why' and 'what now?'!
- Choosing (and sometimes struggling to find) words to express what has been learned ie making generalisations about the experiences and abstracting what it has meant for her.

But we know that learning cannot take place in isolation. Our ideas may come from hearing others talk about theirs, and we may modify them to fit our own viewpoints. Or we may take a completely opposite stance - a perspective we did not know we had until we heard what someone else thought. We can hold a particular belief until another person, speaking to us about their view, actually extends our thinking, and we modify our original thought in the process. Shaping, reshaping, adapting, modifying - all take place in the context of interactive communication. For children, the content has to have meaning and purpose. When children are engaged in the type of talk in which the outcome really matters to them and the purposes for the talk are clear, then not only are there opportunities for the speaker to learn through talk but the listeners too are engaged in active participation. For the children, some of the outcomes of this approach are:

• The need to appreciate and understand one's audience.

• The importance of having precise, clearly defined aims and outcomes.
• The importance of active listening.
• Appreciating that there may be several ways to reach a goal.
• The need for a systematic approach to the investigation.
• Discussion skills, ie making a comment which follows the previous speaker's remarks, being supportive of each other, having sensitivity to group members etc.
• The ability to work in small groups independently.
• The ability to question each other constructively.

However, none of these are possible without the creation of a positive climate in which openness and trust can grow. This is built up slowly, and at times painfully, over a period of time. The overriding aim is to enable children to realise that in school, as in life, the most effective learning is when one is motivated to learn for oneself and that this can be enhanced through communication with others. The most natural medium is talk.

A cross-curricular approach

The children with whom I worked to develop talking as a means of learning and who feature in the activities were familiar with a thematic, cross-curricular approach. Over a period of several years, the staff had involved the children more and more in the selection and planning of a class investigation. Therefore they were increasing their understanding of learning through a process where the planning process was a shared enterprise, teacher and children becoming involved in negotiating ideas, each contributing suggestions and making collaborative decisions. It takes a great deal of confidence to allow children to pursue lines of enquiry which lie outside the teacher's planned programme. This does not imply that he relinquishes his professional responsibility. The major difference between what we plan for children and what they plan for themselves is the purpose of the activity. Children following their own specific investigations (and this is different from being left 'to do your own project') are motivated by a clear purpose defined by them. In seeking the solutions to the questions and problems they themselves pose, there will be a need to acquire new skills as well as to practise those more familiar to them. Skill acquisition, specifically in oracy, takes on new meaning when the context has meaning for the children. Talk then becomes vital and alive, participants become active members, not passive receivers, who can actually influence what goes on in the classroom.

Effective primary education has grown from an understanding of how children learn namely through engaging them in raising questions and encouraging a problem-solving approach to find solutions. There are three crucial aspects of active learning:

- attentiveness
- receptiveness
- appropriateness.

All three elements are present in those institutions in which children understand the purpose of the activities they engage in, have an idea of the desired outcome and are motivated to find ways of achieving the

Children following their own investigations are motivated by a clear purpose.

goal. When children are engaged in situations which really matter to them then the learning which takes place can be of a much higher order than when they undertake tasks supplied by the teacher to develop a narrow range of skills. The activities which follow contain many different starting points. Yet they all have common aims:

- To encourage children to see the purpose of the activity.
- To ensure, whenever possible, that there is a genuine outcome.
- To develop talk as a means of learning.
- To encourage interaction between the children leading towards co-operative group work and decision making.

For these aims to be fostered, I looked at the well-established daily news or 'Show and Tell' sessions with five- to six-year-olds.

I realised that I had to get away from the limited talk of a child simply relating his news to me with the rest of the class passively (or restlessly) listening.

If talk and the purpose of talk are stuck in this mode, then children are being deprived of the type of talk which allows them to debate, question, reflect and become engaged in their own learning. So it was this area which I tackled first - setting goals which were achievable, manageable and on a small scale. The implications from the outcomes were later to affect all other areas of the curriculum. Changes made were not at all original or inspirational. Instead of me asking questions of the speaker, I began to say:
'Does anyone have a question to ask David?'
'Has anyone else had an experience like that? What were your feelings?'
'How do you think she explained that? Does anyone have a puzzle about it?'

When there were obvious gaps between the speaker's appreciation of the audience and the listeners' understanding of what

was being said, it was an ideal opportunity for me to intervene with a comment which helped the speaker to realise that a fuller description was required. She would come to appreciate that assumptions could not be made about the audience's ability to comprehend the speaker's experiences. Events, happenings and thoughts had to be made more explicit and adapted to the listeners' needs.

Interaction now occurred between child and child without me acting as the sole organiser of the talk and the type of discussion was at a greater depth than before. The speaker was having to work much harder in responding to the listeners' comments, and the talk was purposeful. Once I had built up my confidence in giving greater responsibility to the children in directing the discussion, and having seen the value of developing their sensitivity to one another in the way comments were made, I took the next step towards involving them in the planning and direction of the class theme.

Mirror, mirror on the wall - A visit to Oxford City Centre (five- to six-year-olds)

The children had been fascinated by reflections from a series of mirrors set up on display. We were reminded of the ceiling made entirely from mirrors in the Clarendon Centre, Oxford and decided to make a visit there. From the start, I was determined to encourage the children to begin to talk through the arrangements for getting to Oxford City Centre. Genuine problems had to be faced and discussed:

• There is only one minibus which holds 14 people. There are 27 of us. How can we arrange it so that everyone can go?
• How much is it going to cost?

Finding the solution to this meant working out on a scale map how far the

A display of mirrors reminded the children of the mirrored ceiling in the Clarendon Centre, Oxford.

The children made the arrangements themselves to visit the Clarendon Centre, Oxford.

journey would be, enquiring how many miles could the minibus go on one gallon (pre-litre era) and sharing that cost between the children (pre-charging policy era).

Working out the route involved caused much heated discussion. Most of the children were familiar with the difficulty of getting into the city centre and subsequent parking problems. Various relatives' driveways were offered as parking places for the minibus. Finally, the multi-storey car park was chosen as being the most convenient location. Unfortunately, when we arrived there, we realised the minibus was too high to get under the barrier and the talk which followed was focused upon the thoughtlessness of the planners.

This small-scale project took the class a long way forward in terms of planning for an event which actually happened. The seating plans they made for the minibus, the selection of which children to go on which visit and talking through the timings of when to leave and what time to return - all created conditions necessary for active learning and involvement. Yet it did not happen easily. There were many points at which the children became unsure of what

to do. Being inexperienced in this kind of thinking and discussion, and being so young, they could not always see the consequences of a certain course of action. Often you can allow them to experience in reality the outcome of a decision but it would have been unwise to let them have a picnic in the middle of the Clarendon Centre! At this stage, too, the children found it difficult to think through another person's idea or modify their own. As a general rule, if a child had a particular viewpoint, she was determined to prove the legitimacy of that viewpoint at all costs even in the face of evidence proving the contrary. Nevertheless, motivation was high and the children had begun to experience responsibility and independence through talk.

From moo to you - A visit to a dairy (seven-year-olds)

An invitation was received from a parent of one of the children in the class to visit the dairy where she had just started work. Before we went on the visit there were several class discussions concerned with the following questions:

• What do we already know about dairies?
• What do we want to find out?
• How can we find it out?
• Where can we go for help or who might be able to help?
• What are we going to do with our discoveries?
• What sort of activities can we do?

Many of the outcomes were recorded in a variety of ways to give us a focus for future discussions, and so that we could chart the progress of the investigation. Among the concepts, skills, knowledge and attitudes which I highlighted for particular emphasis during the term were these for language development:

• To encourage a willingness to discuss in pairs/in small groups/in class.
• To develop an ability to ask questions and to interview.
• To encourage the use of specific vocabulary related to the theme.
• To use talk as a means of estimating, speculating and hypothesising.

Formulating prior to the visit some questions which were a direct result of examining our existing knowledge and noticing the gaps, meant that the new knowledge could be assimilated in a meaningful way. Questioning, interviewing, describing, informing, recalling and clarifying were experienced by the children in the course of the project and resulted in a dramatic presentation of the production line at the dairy. One interesting point arose from the interviewing of the dairy staff by a child. The child had taken along on the visit a list of questions. At the dairy, the children were given an informative talk and in fact, many of the questions were answered. However, the child still insisted on asking all the questions even though he had found out the majority of the answers. Flexibility in approach and the ability to adapt one's methods of communication to present circumstances comes with practice, confidence and experience. There was no

A visit to a dairy farm involved a great deal of discussion.

doubt that the children learned much about this particular industry, and the interdependence of different groups of people in the production of milk from farmer to milkman, but it was the way in which the children acquired that information that, held for me the greatest significance. In the debates about how answers could be found to new questions in working out, for example, fair tests for discovering the type of milk with the best keeping qualities, children participated in discussions with enthusiasm. However, they soon realised that in order for them to be active participants they actively had to listen and that listening would enable them to develop the discussion from the previous speaker's comments. Sophisticated skills indeed, but ones which some of the children gradually began to acquire.

Sausages or fish fingers? - Planning an overnight stay at a residential camp (seven-year-olds)

A major aspect of this project was the need to plan, buy and organise the cooking of an evening meal, a breakfast and a packed lunch for the whole class plus adult helpers. In small groups of up to four, the children were beginning to take responsibility for initial discussions and then report their findings back to the whole class for further debate. Strategies for finding out the fairest way to determine what people would or would not like to eat, implications of cost, care of preparation and practical issues such as storage, all had to be talked through and negotiated. Sample menus were devised, graphs made to show favourite foods and questionnaires constructed to ensure that throughout the stay each child would be able to eat something at each meal. In the event, quantities were slightly inaccurate at supper as we discovered there were insufficient sausages for two children. The planners, however, were convinced that two of the children must have changed their minds and had sausages instead!

In this particular example, much negotiating had to take place between the planners of the meals, those responsible for the money aspect and those who were going to help buy and prepare the food. Children's personal preferences had to be adapted to a group decision (eg it would have been unworkable to have ten different types of cereal for breakfast). Alternative courses of action had to be devised when it was discovered that one of the menus selected would have taken most of an afternoon to prepare. What the children were discussing was of great importance to them. They knew that calculations needed to be as accurate as possible. They realised, also, that sensitivity to others' preferences or dislikes was necessary if all were to gain

The organising and cooking of the evening meal for an overnight stay caused much negotiation and debate.

pleasure from the experience of being away together. The content of the discussion was highly relevant, but what they were really learning about was people as individuals becoming an harmonious group.

Guinea pigs and car washes

The visit to the classroom of two guinea pigs for a day determined the children's resolve to have some of their own in school. But where to get the money for the cage and upkeep? A long whole class debate ensued. By chance the class were following an investigation into 'garages'. Visits had been made to a local garage, various odd parts from vehicles had been collected and a repair and body shop set up in the classroom. Children working in the class garage took on roles of mechanics, manager, clerk, canteen staff - indeed, they had written their own job descriptions and re-enacted what they had observed on their visits. In the middle of the debate about money for guinea pig cages, one child suggested that the garage could be extended to include a car washing service and the cash received would buy what was needed. This idea led us into a whole new area of discussion:

- What would be a fair price?
- How shall we get customers?
- How do you wash a car properly?
- What about people who want their car polished?

Decisions had to be made about:

- Teams of car washers
- Suitable times for car washing
- Devising an appointments system
- Advertising
- Book-keeping.

Posters were put up all around the school, handbills given to parents, the primary adviser was offered a special rate and even the headteacher was called back from secondment. Instructions cards showing a step-by-step guide to car washing were made by the children and

training sessions were given by the older children. Once the money was collected, a group of children visited a local school which boasted a luxury home for guinea pigs.

Measurements were taken, plans drawn and requests for timber sent to the local DIY shops. Working from the children's plans, a parent gave up three days of his holiday to help groups construct the cage. Towards the end of term, two baby guinea pigs were introduced to their new home.

From this description, it is clear that much more than talk was involved in the project. Other areas of language were automatically employed, as well as maths and craft. Yet again, the greatest benefits derived from this child-initiated project were the experiences and skills they gained through exploring in reality the world of work. Team work, co-operation, problem-solving, organising resources, working towards a desired goal, creating a team spirit were key factors in the sustaining of the children's interest and high motivation, rather than just learning about learning and the processes involved.

Much talk was involved in arranging a car washing service to raise money to buy some guinea pigs.

Which castle? - A consumer survey to find the best castle to visit (seven-to-eight-year-olds)

This investigation took place in the autumn term with a group of children of which two-thirds had been in my class for more than two and a half years. They were becoming increasingly able to discuss, debate, raise questions, accept challenges and become independent in group work. A whole term had been spent in exploring in depth the qualities required for successful group work and ways in which group members could support each other in working through tasks. Awareness had been raised of the skills involved and targets towards which each individual could aim. Co-operative group skills are complex and require much maturity and experience.

Before the term began, I had already decided that, in order to achieve a balance across the year as a whole, I would need to develop an historical aspect. Discussion with the children in the previous term about their interests had revealed a generally common interest in castles. Just how much responsibility the children could undertake in the development of the project was something I wished to investigate. Specific areas of knowledge and understanding, skills objectives and certain attitudes I wanted to develop were selected and recorded and, in relation to oracy, I chose the following as being the most appropriate for this age group:

- asking when and why did it happen?
- asking how we know it is true,
- being willing to take an active part in making plans and offering ideas,
- co-operating with others in negotiating a course of action.

The starting point was a class brainstorm on what the children would like

After a great deal of investigation Warwick Castle was selected for a visit.

to investigate and the likely activities which might ensue. There was a very strong feeling for making a visit to a castle and this become the focus of the discussion and planning for about five weeks.

Pamphlets and brochures were sent for and collected from castles which the children knew as well as ones outside their experience. A list of criteria was drawn up as to what made a good castle to visit from the children's point of view. Groups of children then matched the information in the brochures to the criteria and the 'winning' castle was selected: Warwick. Discussions then took place to decide on cost, transport, timings, letters to parents, booking a coach, arrangements for the day etc. All the jobs that had to be done were displayed on the wall, but they needed putting in some kind of order of priority. A group of eight-year-olds offered to undertake this job. I gave them a room next to the classroom in which to work and I also set up a tape recorder to monitor the type and level of discussion which took place. The task was complex and I wanted to know how decisions were made. After an hour the group reported that they had achieved an order, so another small group was sent in to them to hear the report and to question the first group's reasoning behind a particular order of priorities. When I replayed the tape, I was amazed at the discussion skills displayed and the mature attitude of the children. For two and a half hours (with a 20 minute break) the group remained on task as they coped with speculation, hypothesis, ambiguities, justifying a point of view, adapting an initial idea in the light of further evidence, giving opinions, clarifying, explaining, decision making. The crucial factor seemed to be that the group knew its decisions would be acted upon, that what it was

Engaging in group discussions can improve social skills.

discussing really mattered and would ultimately affect what happened on the day of the visit. The children experienced the difficulty of reaching a compromise, of coping with a member of a group who did not initially make a contribution, of making one's own idea explicit enough for others to understand, of justifying one's decision to another group and of either amending the plan or giving further evidence to support the final outcome. One group member in particular came through as having well-advanced leadership qualities which had not been apparent in the class situation. Gareth was very aware that Christopher was not taking an active part in the group's work. Everytime Christopher was asked 'What do you think, Christopher?' he invariably replied 'Well, I agree with you two'. After a while, Gareth obviously felt that more effort was required and after receiving the same reply for the third time, Gareth asked 'OK, you say you agree, but about what?'

'Well, with what you just said,' replied Christopher.

'But what is it that you agree with? What did we say that you think is good?'

Finally, Christopher had to justify his own reasoning for the decision but until he did so, it would appear that Gareth would not have allowed the discussion to go further. It was achieved with sensitivity, no ill temper, just calm, firm persistence. That such skills were evident in such a young child when many of us are still trying to achieve them after almost 20 years of teaching, is remarkable. It is also significant that after Gareth's gentle persistence, Christopher took a much greater part in the group discussions. Social learning was evident in this activity, as were perseverance, tolerance, open-mindedness and a willingness to be flexible. In describing to the second group what decisions had been made, Gareth discovered an anomaly in the ordering of two items - a costing for the day had to be worked out before a quote had been received from the coach company. This was not evident until he had to explain to another group which had not been part of the decision making. Therefore, he spoke in a much more explicit manner and the actual act of talking highlighted the error. Because his group had made a number of assumptions and had not talked everything through fully, and because they believed all members of the group understood what the others meant, the mistake was made. Teaching some one else can make our own learning much more effective, but how often do we give children this opportunity?

Early years or early stages?

Having recently moved to another school, and now working with nine- to eleven-year-olds who have not had as much experience in using talk for learning as the younger children described above, I am convinced that it is not always helpful to think in terms of age ranges when planning activities. It is more a question of breadth and length of experience. My new class is having to deal with exactly the same difficulties that the five- and six-year-olds had when working through tasks which required co-operative discussion.

Perhaps in some ways it is more difficult for the older children, because their attitudes and their normal patterns of working are so much more entrenched. Introducing open-ended tasks, group work, class discussion, reporting back sessions and planning meetings has had a number of benefits in creating interest, motivation and depth of study, and giving genuine purpose to activities. The learning of skills in terms of how to put forward an idea in a class discussion, how to make constructive criticism, how to listen actively to others and how to make a comment which moves the debate forwards have proved difficult for the children and, in some respects, have created problems with relationships. Children used to working on individual tasks have found the challenges of co-operating, negotiating and taking responsibility for a course of action daunting and somewhat time-consuming at times. Their ability to question, report and think through problems logically has just begun to develop after two terms. The first introduction to involving them in planning and using talk as a means to learning about processes proved problematical. In response to my question 'What would you like to find out about sheep and wool?', a child stated 'If we don't know anything about it in the first place, how do we know what we don't know?'. This was a very logical comment. The fact that they did already possess some knowledge was unrecognised (or at least was not seen to have value one of the first major tasks) was to develop the children's sense of their own worth and to value their existing experience as a basis from which to start. Changes in attitude take considerable energy and time.

With these older children who were in the early stages of becoming involved in their own learning, planning a class assembly proved to be a useful challenge. Ideas for items to be included were brainstormed, possible presenters suggested and group reports drafted. What the children had to learn was the need to adapt the content and mode of presentation to an audience who had no shared experience of the class theme. Talking with one's own class who had been on the same visits and undertaken the same type of activity as oneself meant that various assumptions could be made. Not so with the school audience. A number of difficulties arose which underlined the children's inexperience.

● A group nominated to order the assembly items arbitrarily crossed out a number of children who had volunteered to present something. There was no logic in the selection and the selecting out was done by one child in the group who did not consult with the rest of its members. She was surprised by the reaction of the class when the final ordering did not include those items which had been suggested.
● Some children did not appreciate the need to make adjustments in the use of language and the ways of explaining for much younger children.
● Even in the rehearsal, several children were unable to listen to each other, as if

they had no sense of the team effort required.

In the event, the children rose to the occasion and they presented themselves extremely well. After the assembly we reflected upon:

● What went well?
● What was not so successful?
● How would we do it differently next time?
● What have we learned from the experience?

In the discussion it was evident that their awareness of the skills required had been heightened by the experience and they were delighted by the positive feedback from the audience. It had been a relevant, purposeful, but at times rather painful learning process.

Children will greatly benefit from the opportunity to discuss, plan and organise their own projects.

Talking to learn and the National Curriculum

In all the policy documents so far available the importance of effective communication and practical application is stressed time and time again. The final orders for English include the following goals for speaking and listening (May 1989):

• Development of ability in 'describing experiences, expressing opinions, articulating personal feelings' (Key Stage 1).
• Development of the skills of organising or sequencing information.
• Provision for pupils to talk and listen in groups of different sizes and to a range of audiences through informal and indirect means. Development of the ability to work collaboratively in groups.

The final document in the Science Curriculum includes in the programme of study many references to the importance of

developing reporting skills 'ideally by talking', but also by other means, as appropriate. The raising and answering of questions, collaborative discussions and group work also feature in the programmes of study. Co-operation, the use of children's own questions as starting points and talking through strategies for solving problems are important qualities recognised in the Mathematics document. Examination of the attainment targets gives a more exercise-practising tone. Each segment of the English document on speaking and listening could be easily turned into an activity card, decontextualised and practised until the child has mastered the skill. Here is the greatest danger of the National Curriculum - that teachers will teach to the attainment targets and take the content from the different levels. Preventing this from happening depends upon our full appreciation of how children learn most effectively. If we take the programmes of study as the base and highlight for ourselves the words contained there such as 'by informal and indirect means', 'in the course of purposeful activities', 'from across the curriculum', etc then the requirements of the National Curriculum could still be met through the projects and investigations described here.

Implications for the teacher

At a time when the teacher is being asked both to come to terms with new terminology, new concepts and new content revealing, in many cases, gaps in knowledge and understanding, and also to become familiar with proposals for testing, assessment and reporting, it is understandable if he believes that effective primary practice has also to change to meet the requirements. I have attempted to show how the challenges can be accomplished through investigations which are realistic, which are important to the children and which encompass several areas of the curriculum. Talk which is purposeful, which directs thought, forms opinion, creates ideas and courses of action, which is used to reflect upon and interpret experience, is also one of the most powerful tools for learning - both content and process, both about oneself and about other people. Talk has been and will remain the most natural form of communication. What the National Curriculum will do, however, is to underline its central function and importance and to widen the range of purposes and situations for which it is used. Some changes in teachers' roles will, however, be inevitable but these can be positive rather than negative ones. Among the most important I would include:

● The need for the teacher to have precise, concise, achievable goals for the children in terms of language skills, attitudes, knowledge and understanding of concepts.

● The need for children and teacher to negotiate and debate the direction for the investigation and its planning.
● Where the teacher has a legitimate reason for introducing a particular topic, there is greater importance in encouraging the children to raise questions, consider possible sources of information and suggest activities.
● The importance of the teacher having clear goals yet also having flexibility of approach in order to use unforeseen circumstances to develop discussion and collaborative group work.
● Having high expectations of the children in terms of what they can achieve given involvement, motivation and clear understanding of the purpose of the activity.
● Encouraging reflection and self-assessment through talk as a class and on a one-to-one basis with peer or adult. Only by this means can new targets be set for the next time a similar situation is experienced.
● Working with colleagues to devise realistic monitoring systems to:
1 record areas of experience;
2 record achievements of individual pupils;
3 ensure whole-school approaches and policies.

This is in itself a problem-solving activity requiring negotiation, co-operation, creativity and skills of oral communication at an adult level. Certainly an activity which demands learning through talk.

It may be important to point out, in conclusion, that any change which you may be contemplating in terms of talk in the classroom should be a manageable one.

It will take time to develop and longer still for results to become apparent. It will demand skilful management of the group situation to allow purposeful talk to develop and it may be necessary to discuss in explicit terms what skills are required to make a group discussion successful. Yet time well spent in the early stages will reap many benefits later and in other areas of the curriculum. What the children will be experiencing will be the process of learning itself and there can be little else of greater educational value than that.

Talk in project work
David Wray

Talk in project work
David Wray

INTRODUCTION

Almost all primary teachers involve their children in some form of project or thematic work. There is obviously a great deal of variation in the extent of this work, with some teachers basing almost their entire curriculum upon it, and others arranging their work so that 'basic skills' such as language, reading and mathematics are taught separately. There is also great variation in methods of organising this kind of work. In some classes project work is a whole-class activity, with children all doing the same activities at the same time, while in others it is an individual activity, and children are allowed to follow their own personal lines of enquiry. Of course, there are many other arrangements between these two.

Given the large degree of variation which exists in the practice of project work, it is, perhaps, not very surprising that it has given rise to increasing concern in recent years. Concern has been expressed over the relationship between project work and the concept of curriculum balance, particularly in the light of new developments in curriculum planning and the introduction of a National Curriculum. Concern has also been expressed over the content of project work, and its effectiveness as a context for children's learning. It has been caricatured, somewhat unfairly in many cases, as 'uninvolved copying', and doubt has been expressed over the extent of children's learning through it.

The aim of this chapter is to explore the possibilities for beneficial talking and listening in project work.

Of course, it would be very unusual for a piece of project work to be done in a primary class without there being a great deal of talking and listening involved. Talk is basic to the process of doing a project, as it is to most activities in the primary school. The point from which this chapter begins, however, is that the learning potential of talk in project work may be under-used unless specific plans are made to capitalise upon it. The chapter then focuses particularly upon the planning of project work and the role of talk within it.

The project process

For a project to be of maximum benefit it needs to be both purposeful and systematic. To be purposeful implies that it is well planned, and features of this planning, focused on the inclusion of opportunities for talk, are discussed on page 96. It also requires an organisational system which allows participants to keep track of where they are in the process. One means of such organisation is described here, set into the context of one particular project which was carried out with third year junior school children.

The system involves four stages, each of which should involve teacher and children working together, rather than the teacher simply imposing ideas upon the children.

The project was called 'Holidays' and arose through interest generated in the class by the children's sharing of their plans for holidays during the coming vacation. Not all the activities undertaken are described, but sufficient to give a flavour of the approach.

Devising goals

First of all the children, under the guidance but not the domination of the teacher, decided what they hoped to achieve during the project. (It was felt important to give the children as much responsibility for planning and running the project as possible. Their commitment was felt to be crucial if the aim of setting skill teaching within a meaningful context was to be achieved.) Two of the goals specified were

The children visited local post offices to get passport application forms.

for the children to produce their own holiday brochures for places they had visited, and their own passports.

Making plans

The teacher and pupils then went on to decide how to set about achieving the specified aims. They decided that they would have to obtain examples of holiday brochures as well as other information about specific holiday areas. This involved making arrangements to visit travel agents as well as the local and school libraries. They also decided that a real passport would be needed, and after some discussion one of the children offered to bring in his mum's! Plans were made to visit local post offices to ask for passport application forms. Eventually enough of these were obtained to enable each child to fill one in (for practice). All the tasks were delegated and working groups established, each with a timetable within which their particular tasks should be completed. The children were given the freedom to choose their own pattern of working through the various tasks they had to do, and also who they preferred to work with.

Implementing plans

In carrying out the plans that had been made the children then had to exercise a whole range of location and selection skills. They obtained information from books and other printed materials and also by asking questions of people. They physically went to the places where the information they wanted could be found, in libraries, post offices or travel agents. They then obtained the information and brought it back to school. Then they evaluated the information they had, and put it together into an appropriate form. They filled in forms (monitoring each other to ensure they did it correctly), designed their passports, and joined together descriptive prose and appropriate pictures to produce holiday brochures which presented information in

They also visited travel agents to obtain information.

an accurate and attractive way. All these activities were done with the benefit (and sometimes the hindrance) of peer advice.

Evaluating progress

The children and the teacher continually evaluated the success of the process. Regular sessions were held in which groups reported back on their progress. Their form-filling was monitored by other children, and those responsible for obtaining things like printed brochures from travel agents were under a good deal of pressure from their classmates to deliver the goods on time. At the end of the project other children were allowed to read the finished brochures and were asked their opinions as to whether these gave sufficient information to enable a choice of holiday resort to be made, and also whether they presented the resorts in a suitably attractive light.

Criticisms were taken seriously by the authors, several of whom subsequently asked if they could work further on their

pieces to improve them in the light of these criticisms.

During the project there were several opportunities for instruction in information skills, particularly those of evaluating and synthesising information from a range of sources. Occasionally groups got together who were having similar problems, and direct instruction was given. Twice the whole class was brought together for some work on critical reading, using a selection of advertisements and newspaper reports. On many more occasions invidual children's difficulties were highlighted and attempts made to deal with them on the spot, using a variety of resources. Commercially produced books of exercises on such topics as 'using an index', or 'skimming' were found very useful for this. It was felt that this sort of instruction given during the project was more likely to have lasting effect because it was set within a meaningful context. Children could, it was felt, see a purpose in this instruction simply because it was helping them achieve better results in a project in which they were very interested.

The role of talk

Productive talk in project work is most beneficial if it is planned in from the beginning, although of course there will always be a place for spontaneous talk and much learning to be derived from it.

The teacher and the whole class

A great deal of discussion will take place between the teacher and the class, especially at the beginning of a project. One of the very first tasks for the teacher is to discuss the topic thoroughly with the class in order to ascertain what they already know about it. This kind of discussion needs little special guidance from the teacher, who can allow things to follow more or less along lines chosen by the class. It has two main functions. Firstly it gives the teacher an idea of the present knowledge of the class so that she can know the points on which the project might focus in order to

extend this knowledge. This is important because project work will clearly stimulate children more and have greater learning benefit if the children feel they are actually 'finding out' new things.

The second function of the preliminary discussion is to bring the children's previous knowledge about a topic to the forefront of their minds. Current theories about learning suggest that for new learning to take place efficiently there not only have to be previous ideas for this new learning to connect to, but these previous ideas have to be activated so that they are readily available in the learner's memory for connections to be made. Discussion therefore can not only stimulate the children but can also assist the process of learning which is to come.

A special kind of discussion will also take place between the teacher and the class towards the beginning of a project. This can be termed 'negotiation' and it is crucial in really beneficial project work. Although one of the chief benefits of project work is that it allows learning to follow children's interests, most teachers will recognise that children's interests:

• tend to be rather ephemeral unless developed and nurtured by a teacher,
• generally do not include learning many things which the teacher wants them to learn, which often seem abstract to children.

By negotiation with children at the beginning of a project the teacher can:

• help them to see longer term interest in what they plan to do,
• build into the project a combination of her aims and theirs,
• ensure that they both feel committed to the project and will be engaged in real learning.

The first thing that will need to be discussed is what exactly the project will involve, and what its end-products will be. Both the teacher and the children will have ideas about this, and together they will have to produce a set of feasible goals. It is little use the teacher running this discussion by

making statements such as 'We are going to… '. Statements such as 'We could…' are far more likely to persuade children that they can have a say in planning the project, and they can also use this tentative form of expression for suggesting their own ideas.

This same kind of discussion will also be useful in deciding how the project will be broken down into smaller units. A typical way of organising a project is to begin with an umbrella topic, such as 'Trains', and then to break this down into sub-topics, such as 'The history of the railways', 'How trains work' etc, each of which becomes the special responsibility of one group of children. Through negotiation the children can be involved in this breaking down, and the discussion may reveal a great deal about the structure of their existing ideas about the topic.

A third area for negotiation concerns the composition of the working groups and the physical arrangements for the project. By having to articulate reasons why they should work with particular other children (beyond the 'he's my friend' argument) and why they should spend every afternoon for a term on the project, for example, children

A project such as 'China' can be sub-divided into smaller units of study.

are encouraged to follow through the logic of their arguments and consider how they fit with other demands. This kind of talk (sustaining an argument) is one they generally get little experience of in the classroom.

Within working groups

If the work on a project involves a large proportion of group work then a great deal of talk will take place between members of the group. It is important to note, however, that simply putting children into groups will not necessarily lead to a great deal of productive group talk. Studies of group operation in the classroom eg Galton, Simon & Croll (1980) and Tann (1981) have suggested that things are more complex than this. Much 'group work' seems to consist of groups of individuals each pursuing their own private tasks and interacting with each other chiefly about non-work matters. The key fact which seems to transform this situation is the engagement of groups in collaborative tasks, that is, tasks whose completion depends upon co-operation between members of the group. Project work can be ideally suited to this.

One of the first tasks of the group, having decided which area of the project they will concentrate upon, is to agree upon the actual work they will do and how it will be organised. This can be done with or without the teacher, although, if children have little experience of this kind of discussion, they may benefit from having a teacher show them the appropriate kinds of talk. This talk will include brainstorming as a way of generating ideas, exploration of links between ideas, negotiation of precise responsibilities, planning of activities, and, above all, the establishment of commitment among the participants in these planned tasks.

While the project is underway, if the groups are genuinely collaborating, there will also need to be regular discussion between them. This is in addition to the inevitable talk which takes place between members of a group as they pursue tasks

Individual groups have to agree on the work they will do.

together; commenting upon each other's ideas, exploring ideas together, helping each other with particular activities, sharing and commenting upon resources, jointly composing notes, stories, factual writing etc, and generally supporting each other in their agreed tasks.

More formal talk, time for which may need to be planned in, will include individuals or sub-groups informing their colleagues about the work they have done, elaborating points on which they are having problems, outlining immediate future plans and responding to questions. Other members of the group will listen and make helpful comments or criticisms on the work which has been done, offer their own ideas to support, extend or contradict those they hear, and discuss how the work of the group as a whole is progressing and fitting together. It is particularly valuable if children ask questions of their peers (beyond the straightforward factual questions such as What did you do then?) Questions which demand in response explanation (Why did ...?), speculation (What if...?) and exploration of ideas (What does this mean?) seem to give rise to significant learning, both for the children who try to answer the questions and for those who are grappling with ideas enough to ask them.

This kind of talk is only more formal in the sense that it may require the earmarking of particular sessions in which it can take place. Perhaps once a week the group can be asked to spend some time on a review session, which the teacher can attend, but contributing only when specifically asked to. This session can also be valuable rehearsal time for other regular 'sharing' sessions at which groups discuss their work so far with the rest of the class.

Between working groups and the class

Regular discussion between working groups and the rest of the class will, apart from having benefits in terms of purposeful talk,

Regular discussions between working groups is essential.

also serve as a means of keeping the class together during their project work. In a project involving several sub-groups working on distinct areas it is easy for the project to lose its unity, and the teacher needs to have a policy for bringing things together at regular intervals. One of the best means of doing this is to have a regular sharing or review time at which each group reports back to the rest of the class on the work which they have been doing. Apart from providing opportunities for useful talking and listening this also gives the teacher valuable information to enable some assessment of children's progress, or points on which further information is needed for this assessment.

Obviously, these reports require some prior preparation. (They also require some work to have been done!) They are thus a valuable but unobtrusive way of motivating children to meet targets for their work. Each group will need some time before each review session to plan together what they will report to the class. This planning time also serves the purpose of clarifying things for the group itself.

After hearing a group's report the rest of the class could ask questions about anything which they do not understand or would like further information about, or make suggestions as to how the group's work might be extended, refined or otherwise improved. The teacher should stress that comments such as these should be positive and helpful rather than destructive. The group could then try to answer the questions they have been asked, or respond to the comments. This should open up a general discussion about the group's progress from which several useful ideas may emerge, including some targets for the group to deal with immediately.

Clearly in sessions like this the teacher's role is very important. The teacher will, in fact, be modelling the behaviour which the children will copy. This behaviour therefore needs to be appropriate and helpful. It is likely to be most helpful if it consists of such things as:

- listening attentively, without interrupting, to what individuals have to say;
- responding to statements seriously and helpfully;
- offering suggestions rather than prescriptions for future actions;
- giving clear reasons why ideas are agreed or disagreed with.

Between working groups and the teacher

During the course of the project the teacher will be fully involved in the work of the children. This may include some direct teaching of the class, of groups and of

The teacher needs to be fully involved with the groups.

The teacher can join in with the groups as they try to solve problems through discussion.

individuals, as in the example given earlier. A majority of the teacher's time, however, will probably be spent working with the groups as they pursue their project assignments. There is scope for a great deal of talking and listening here.

The teacher can question and probe the work the groups are doing, inviting explanations and justifications. By having to explain what they are doing or about to do, children in the group develop an increased awareness of their activities and become alert to new possibilities and directions. The teacher can also model the role of interested listener.

The teacher can join in with the group as an equal partner as they attempt to solve particular problems through discussion. This is perhaps the hardest role of all for teachers to adopt, as they may know perfectly well what the solution to a problem is, and may find it very difficult

indeed not to impose their understanding upon children who are not yet ready, and who will learn best through making their own mistakes. Being an equal partner in a group means having no more right to have correct solutions than any other member. It does not mean that these viewpoints cannot be expressed, but simply that if they are rejected by the rest of the group the teacher has to accept this, just as a child would.

The teacher may also, of course, adopt a more teacherly role in group discussion, especially as the project nears its completion. The discussion can be steered towards a consideration of what the precise form of the final outcome will be. A version of this will probably have been agreed at the beginning of the project, but the work which has been done and the information which has been collected may mean a re-negotiation of the end-product. The teacher can help the group iron out exactly what they will produce, and how it will be presented. This again means listening to the children rather than imposing ideas, but also helping them to see possible problems with their ideas. Thinking things through may come about through group discussion, or it may require the odd idea to be thrown in by the teacher.

Between the class and visitors

Visitors that have particular knowledge about the areas the children are researching can be extremely useful and motivating at any point in a project. Children are also likely to get the opportunity to talk to other people when they themselves are on a visit, for example, when they talk to the curator on a museum visit, or an engine driver on a visit to a railway station. The benefits to be gained from both these situations will be greater if children are prepared beforehand to use the resource effectively.

This preparation will be of two kinds, to fit the two kinds of activities likely to be involved when with the outside expert.

Asking questions

Teachers often express disappointment with the questions their children ask visitors. They may seem banal and uninteresting, and if the children are shy, they may be halting and poorly expressed. This is largely the result of poor preparation. If children are to get the most from the occasion they will need some rehearsal. For the visitor as well, who may be unused to talking to children, a well-prepared group will seem easier to deal with and respond to than one whose interest has to be kept alive. One way of preparing them is as follows.

A few days before the visit, explain to

It is very useful to invite visitors that have particular knowledge about the areas that the children are researching.

the children who they will be talking to, and what kind of interesting things they may be told about. Encourage them to share their previous relevant experiences, and generally try to stimulate their interest. As this develops guide the discussion on to things they would like to find out from the visitor. With younger children the teacher may at this stage jot down on the blackboard some questions which arise.

With slightly older children (juniors) a useful technique is to put them into groups of four to five, and give them perhaps 20 to 30 minutes in which to discuss and formulate some questions they may ask the visitor. Have a class feedback session, and decide on two or three questions each group could ask. Get them to select one favourite question per group which they can ask first, in case time runs out before all the questions are asked.

On the day of the visit remind the class of the questions they talked about, and of what they would like to find out from the visitor. Even with older children it is best not to have them read their questions out from a prepared sheet. This seems unspontaneous and stilted. With younger children it will not work anyway. If the preparation has been done thoroughly as described, the class will remember enough interesting things to ask, and their questions will be more interesting for being more spontaneously worded.

Listening to answers

Most teachers complain at times that their children cannot or will not listen. However, listening to a novel voice telling them things they are interested in hearing is perhaps a situation most likely to result in good listening. Children will, nevertheless, still benefit from some preparatory work, although this is likely to be more long-term in nature.

There are two real prerequisites to children listening well to visitors, and these are simply that they must be interested in what is being said, and they must be capable of understanding most of it. The teacher cannot absolutely ensure either of these, but she can help a great deal along the way. The children's interest can be

The golden rule is to 'prepare' the children for visitors.

stimulated before the visitor arrives by some prior discussion and work on the topic. This is also necessary to ensure that the children know enough about what the visitor will talk about for the content of the talk to make sense to them. Preparation of questions to ask, as already described, will also help.

The golden rule, then, when using visitors is 'Prepare'. It should also be remembered that a great deal of useful practice in asking questions and listening to answers can be gained by using the most common classroom resources of all - each other, and especially the teacher. If children are encouraged to ask and answer questions whenever they are working they will get better at it.

Between the class and special audiences

Many pieces of project work have outcomes which are only shared with other members of the same class, perhaps in one of the 'sharing' times referred to earlier. Others, however, go further than this and aim at some kind of presentation to other audiences. These audiences may range from children in the rest of the school, at a special assembly, for example, to an invited gathering of parents, governors etc.

Presentations of this kind will clearly require children to explain their work to others and to discuss beforehand ways in which it can be made as attractive and informative as possible. Explaining your work to a large audience, many of whom will be strangers, involves a different approach to talk than simply explaining it to your classmates. It also requires a fair degree of rehearsal to ensure that it is intelligible and appropriate. Children's presentations of this kind commonly require a lot more talk to produce than they actually involve on the day!

Another form of presentation is to other children, perhaps in different schools or even different parts of the country, via tape or video recording. Preparing an audio or video tape of work they have done is something children get a great deal of pleasure from but which also involves a lot of talking to purpose.

The following statement sumarises this chapter succinctly - the key to the successful development of talk in project work, and indeed the successful use of project work at all, lies in careful, but flexible, planning.

It is very constructive for children to share their project outcomes in a special assembly.

Talk in science
Clive Carré

Talk in science
Clive Carré

INTRODUCTION

Even at an early age children can learn the complexities of our language, but in doing so they need to take risks. In science especially, error is inherent in this process of 'trying out' new ways of expressing ideas and in using specialist vocabulary. This calls for tolerance on the teacher's part in accepting degrees of correctness in children's talk and in searching behind the words to find the meaning. For example, Tom, a ten-year-old, is telling a teacher about food chains in a river.

Teacher: And where will the weeds get their energy?
Tom: From the soil ... or from the water ... or from the rain or the weather. The rain and probably the sun.

Similarly, two eleven-year-olds are talking about why it is easier to float in the sea than in fresh water.

Pupil 1: Salt ... I think I know ... 'cos in the sea there's all the salt ... it forms a skin ... you can break through it easily but it'll hold you up.
Pupil 2: It gives you more balance ... it's lighter ... it takes the weight away ... it's the pressure of the water.

The inaccuracies and partial understandings demand that further talk should be encouraged. It is important to help the children say what they may know, rather than condemn their statements.

Talk between children and teacher enables them to 'play around with ideas', testing out thoughts and drawing inferences and so on. What we hear may bear little relationship to the complex business of making connections with existing thoughts which is going on inside the head. The internalised mental processes are a bit of a mystery, but Vygotsky (1962) claimed that what at one instance happens as overt speech happens internally at a later stage as thought. He did not claim that mental activity was a direct replica of the words used, but he did argue that its nature was derived from them. A reasonable hypothesis, therefore, is that the social act of talking will assist the development of thinking processes in science. Vygotsky was responsible for the deceptively simple statement that 'Thought is internalised action'; others have qualified this idea. Even though not everyone would agree that language might directly affect intellectual development, there would be agreement that mental activity is derived from action.

Science offers a great deal of opportunity both for 'doing' and for 'talking about' action, and it is not surprising that the National Curriculum ensures that all children will be engaged in science activity.

However, to justify the time and effort spent on the subject it must be more than just engaging in practical work. Practical manipulation of materials, even expensive ones, is not in itself a learning activity. Extensive activity is highly desirable in primary school, but eventually it must help towards changing the learner's understanding. As already pointed out elsewhere (Carré 1981), the effort of 'doing' can be totally ineffective unless pupils have the opportunity to link new experiences with already acquired understandings. Learning by 'doing' is only the first step, reflecting upon that activity is an equally important second step which will help pupils change the way they represent the world to themselves.

One vital role of the teacher is to organise opportunities for children to gain first-hand experience through practical work, and then other opportunities for thinking and talking about what has been going on.

The National Curriculum states the content and process skills needed, but the teachers have to plan how to incorporate these demands imaginatively into the two sets of activities, both 'doing practical work' and 'using language to make sense of what has been experienced'.

What sort of science should be encouraged?

In the adult world, what we think goes on in the heads of scientists when they are engaged in their work is twofold. Science is about two separate things: imagining ideas, and then testing them. Having ideas is the same as forming hypotheses, imaginative guesses of what might be possible, and these are essentially creative activities. The second part is the test, an experiment to see whether the imagined world is anything like reality.

Medawar (1984) explains science succinctly as 'a dialogue between two voices, the one imaginative and the other critical; a dialogue, as I have put it, between the possible and the actual, between proposal and disposal, conjective and criticism, between what might be true and what is in fact the case'.

This also applies to the everyday actions of children and adults. Scientific method can be seen to be an extension of common sense, inventing stories about possible realities, testing and modifying the stories as new experiences are gathered. (A caution is necessary here, for a hypothesis even if imaginatively conceived must be one that could be true or plausible; it cannot be idiotic or a nonsense.)

This makes science a very human form of behaviour, more a set of justifiable beliefs than a compilation of factual 'truths'. If we have a hypothesis that by practical experience (ie testing) we find to work for us, it evolves into a theory. We all have collections of personal theories.

Any personal theory can be shown to be inadequate in new, different circumstances, and if we can no longer rely on it, it needs modification or rejection. Accepting such evidence at times can be quite hard, especially if we are committed to our personal view of what ought to be!

The following is an example of a personal theory evolving. Robert is nine years old and his teacher has asked him to explain why two beer cans suspended close together will bang together if one blows gently between them. He talks at length, thinking through the problem:

Robert: And, oh yea! when you blow, you try to put... or you blow...you blow straight

The teacher and pupil talk through the problem together.

out, and the main blow you do doesn't...it goes straight through without hitting it.
Teacher: Yes.
Robert: And outside bits, they're the ones that hit it, so there's no pressure pushing outwards, it's all pushing it in.
Teacher: Oh!
Robert: Instead of the main part going straight through... 'Cos if it's going to go straight through... the air would hit there, and if it was there it would sort of go in a bit really.
Fifteen minutes later, with great excitement he thinks he's 'got it'.
Robert: Does it depend upon how far apart they are?... the string twisting...the waves of air pushing out from your mouth...the air goes into the grooves on the outside of the can...and knocking it in...because there's a bigger space where the outside can hit...the air points between the can scoops it out sort

of...gravity increases and pulls them together...this might not be true...the molecules of the air were...this is going to sound strange...the molecules will vaporize...and there's no space there...that's my thunder theory.

Notice in this monologue how Robert puts himself at risk, exploring all the science ideas he has come into contact with and having fun using his latest language discoveries in specialist vocabulary. The teacher has not 'corrected' or tried to alter his suggested hypotheses; in fact, the lack of intervention has encouraged Robert to talk through the pictures in his mind, using the metaphor of thunder to represent what he has observed (the two tin cans banging together) in terms of things he knows about in real life (thunder). By way of comparison, a physics graduate explaining part of the same phenomenon does so with the confidence to put his understanding into a flow of words:

'As the air travels over the two curved surfaces, the air molecules are spread out and their effective pressure on the sides of the can, acting here and here [points to inside surfaces of cans] is reduced, because there are less of them on the surface. Hence their effective pressure is less. So, atmospheric pressure acting on the outside is now greater than pressure on the inside and this causes the two cans to be drawn together.'

Behind both personal theories lie particular assumptions and conceptual understandings and particular use of language. Neither theory is 'right' or 'wrong'. [Flow around objects is a complex process. For even the simplest case of turbulent flow there is as yet no method of obtaining a complete mathematical solution.] Theories can never be absolutely right, but they are judged on whether they work or not, and are limited, too, for a particular purpose. If a theory fails to work it is discarded. Also, if it works today it may not work tomorrow, for the world is always changing and theories have to be continually revised.

We can see then that we continually create theories about the small 'bits' of the world we live in and and submit them to testing. In 'real' life, outside the school, the process is called 'learning', and inside the classroom we call it 'experimenting'.

The pupil attempts to explore all the science ideas he knows to find an explanation.

We are all theory makers and testers

It must be stressed that all our understandings, our values and prejudices are based upon personal theories. Without personal theories we cannot make sense of our environment, for they help us to interpret reality against a set of our past experiences. Guy Claxon (1984) emphasises that even our perceptions are products of our personal theories, and that what we do depends on what we consider the world to be. He says:

'Common sense says we see things the way they are, then we make decisions about what's important, and finally we select actions that will get us what we want and avoid what we don't. Common sense is wrong. What we see is an output of our personal theory, not an input to it.'

As Robert has shown, struggling to make sense of a science event, all perceptions are interpretive and are constructed in unique ways. The following example shows how a six-year-old's perception was influenced by all the work he had done on growing things. A colleague reported to me that a visitor, on entering the class, provoked one lad to whisper to his teacher: 'Why is that man's head growing through his hair?'. A unique perspective on a very bald head! So we do not see events in science or in everyday life precisely the way they are, but rather as the way we perceive them to be. Put another way, my actions and speech will depend upon what my personal theories tell me about reality, not what reality is said to be like by 'authority'.

How do children develop their personal theories?

In everyday life, children create theories about everything they do. At an intuitive level they develop theories about things such as the weight of a bucket of water, the force needed to push a cart, the effect of putting substances on the fire, the change in water placed in a refrigerator, and so on.

Gradually, through experience, children evolve practical understanding of their physical world; about gravity, flotation, electricity, force, heat and so on, and they do so in a number of ways.

Personal theories can come from immediate physical experiences such as that the more force one uses to bounce a ball, the greater the height it will bounce back; getting into a bath causes the water to rise; and a helium balloon will float away if you let go of the string.

This sort of learning from experience is basic to understanding because further action can be predicted from it. A child 'knows' that getting into a bath when it is full will cause the water to flow over the top! The important thing to note is that such personal theories require no language at all, but if the use of language can be encouraged, and imagery constructed, then the mental exploration will eventually result in a quicker change in the personal theory than would be the case if no verbalisation were encouraged.

Many personal theories today come from the media, and television in particular

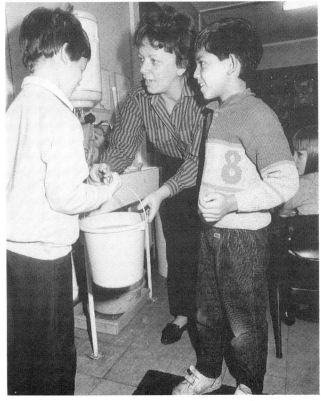

Children try to create theories about everything they do.

provides an endless stream of images.

The juxtaposition of *Superman* with a documentary on the remarkable use of laser beams, *Tomorrow's World* explaining holography and the make-believe world of James Bond makes it difficult sometimes to distinguish 'fact' from 'fiction'. One eight-year-old, on being asked why he thought two magnets were attracted to each other said quickly, 'It's a force-field, Sir!'.

Eric Carle's *The Mixed-up Chameleon* and *The Very Hungry Caterpillar* are examples of texts where imagination is used without restraint. There is obviously no requirement for authors to justify the degree to which their fantasy world deviates from reality. The point to emphasise is that the text may be perceived in the same light as an information book, in which at primary level reality is often portrayed as a series of partial truths and misconceptions. Although many children know about the convention of stories and author's licence, a class of seven-year-olds discussed in a very lively manner how much Eric Carle deviated from their understanding of caterpillars.

Pupil 1: 'How can you have a blue caterpillar with a green and yellow body ... and a red face ... orange feet.'
Pupil 2: 'His eyes are too big.'
Pupil 3: 'There's no antennae on ours ...'
Pupil 4: 'No pupa stage in this book.'
Pupil 5: 'Caterpillars do not eat all bits of things ... do they ... only one sort of food ... like ... and lollipop's too hard to get through ...'

This class of children had developed strong personal theories about caterpillars, based on their own investigations over a term. The teacher was challenging their ideas with a text which some may have accepted as representing reality. Information books for this age range can show misconceptions just as disturbing as those portrayed in Eric Carle's story.

Personal theories cause a problem in teaching science. Each child will view an event from a particular perspective.

A child may have been taught that the sun is at the centre of all planetary orbits, yet still say 'the sun rises in the East and

sets in the West'. The intuitive idea, plausible in medieval times that the sun circles the Earth can coexist with the formal science that has been learned at school. Similarly a personal theory about where the stomach lies, gleaned from 'tummy aches' below the belt, has to coexist with information that the stomach is just below the diaphragm, high in the abdomen.

Fundamental questions need to be posed, based on the ideas outlined, about the sort of science we should be encouraging:

1 Should we help children understand our 'accepted adult view' of the world by giving them opportunities to confirm or verify this sort of knowledge (ie work is planned by the teacher to lead towards chosen patterns of understanding)?
2 Should children be encouraged to engage in the process of being 'real' scientists, and in this role create hypotheses and collaboratively test them in as critical a way as possible (ie a more open approach where children follow their own lines of enquiry)?

Current thinking about science teaching is focusing upon creating an awareness of different teaching styles and having a repertoire from which a choice may be made, to balance the two approaches above.

Eric Carle's 'The Very Hungry Caterpillar' caused much lively discussion.

A repertoire of teaching strategies

The tightness of a teacher's structure

Research indicates that pupils quickly become aware of what is being taught by the way a teacher presents ideas. Your assumptions about the nature of science and what school science should be like are communicated to pupils, intentionally or unintentionally, and will affect their learning.

Here is an example of a young teacher beginning a lesson on volume to a group of eleven-year-old children:

Teacher: Can anyone give me an idea of what volume is?
Pupil 1: It's the stuff inside summat.
Pupil 2: How high things?
Pupil 3: How loud?
Teacher: No, we're not doing that today. Write down 'a volume is the amount of space taken up by a body'.

This teacher justified his neglect of the ideas the pupils had by 'not wanting to waste time'. This approach hardly encourages the pupils in this class to make their own ideas explicit, but the class did get on with things quickly. The teacher's own knowledge established the purpose and direction of the lesson. Understanding of the concept of volume, in his lesson, was thought to be achieved through definition and through the practical work which followed.

The lesson was tightly structured, and presumably the teacher would argue that he is concerned that children are getting 'correct' information. This style is particularly common with teachers who feel unsure about their own understanding of science concepts. Making the pupils guess what's in the teacher's mind is the very opposite approach to exploring the prior knowledge in the heads of the learners.

However, a style can be less teacher-directed, and even within planned activities a teacher can encourage pupils to learn through their own efforts and to alter their personal theories. The following example of classroom talk illustrates a teacher emphasising the specialist vocabulary which the children aged ten to eleven years, have just 'researched'. They have just completed some practical work on melting and dissolving.

Pupil: They've separated.
Teacher: Yes, they've separated, that's a nice word.
Pupil 2: It's dissolved.
Teacher: You think it's dissolved?
Pupil 3: I think it's melted.
Teacher: You think it's melted.
  He refrains from saying the 'right answer' and his further questioning elicits a personal theory of one child, an alternative framework for thinking about the process of dissolving:

Pupil 1: Er...the sugar shrinks in the cup.
Teacher: You mean it gets smaller?
Pupil 1: Yes.
Teacher: How do you know it gets smaller?
Pupil 1: Because it's dissolving in the cup. It gets wet and it...it shrinks.
  Science has an agreed view of public knowledge, and faced with the pupil's view that particles shrink, the teacher needs to draw attention to that personal understanding and help change the child's understanding over time.

Using pictures to talk about the invisible

In a different context, a group of six-year-olds were being taught about melting, and the change of state from solid ice cube to liquid water. In the class discussion one boy volunteered the information that if an ice cube was smashed into smaller and smaller bits, the tiniest bit would be called a molecule. He had heard the word on television. To capitalise on this remarkable use of vocabulary in an appropriate context the pupils were shown the visual representation in *If I Met a Molecule* by N Wilson (Hutchinson, 1970). In this book,

the humanoid molecules, 'wriggle and get excited' and 'get so excited that we escape'. This helped the children to form a mental image of invisible particles in constant motion, and the fact that there is more space than solid in objects as hard as the table tops. In drawing their own versions of events in the imaginary world where the behaviour of invisible particles causes ice to form water and vice versa they used the following language about molecules: 'spread out', 'are packed tight together', 'are free', 'more apart', 'becoming loose', 'stuck together', 'flew around', 'get closer'.

The teacher's role in small groups

Working in groups can create problems, and one research project concluded that teaching children how to work together and help each other appeared to be a totally

Pupils can be encouraged to learn through their own efforts.

neglected art at primary level. The next extract illustrates how talk changes when a teacher enters the group. The responses are more lengthy and are elevated from mere organisational talk. Simon ventures a hypothesis; it is as if the teacher's presence removes the competitiveness to get a word in! These ten-year-olds are trying to find out if different substances dissolve in water, and about factors like stirring that affect the process.

Pupil 1: Yes he has, I can see.
Pupil 2: He has.
Pupil 1: He's got less than Peter.
Pupil 2: Ready ... another ten seconds stirring. Go (counting) ... Stop.
Pupil 1: I've got one in there (argument over microphone) Stop.
Pupil 2: Let's have a look.
Pupil 1: That's it.
Pupil 2: Rachel you stop stirring ... Stop now.
Pupil 1: I've got more left too.
Pupil 2: It's dissolving.
Teacher: Why did it happen, Simon?

Simon: 'Cos er, when Peter put the sand in and stirred it, it didn't go but when er ... put the salt in it did go, because the sand's heavier.
Teacher: I see, OK. Melody, could you come here a minute? What did you notice happened? What was different? The stirrer and the non-stirrer?
Melody: The non-stirrer put the sugar in and er, went to the bottom and er, the one that stirred that, that dissolved, when you stir it for a bit of the time it dissolved.

Children have to be taught how to co-operate and listen to each other.

Encourage children to take the teacher's role

Two eleven-year-olds have been comparing the density of salt water and fresh water. Using a straw hydrometer, they have found out that salt water is denser than fresh water. They are then given a problem to

Children have to be taught how to co-operate and listen to each other.

A project on Plimsoll lines encouraged the children to take the teacher's role.

Country'. Is it empty there too, Mark?
Michelle: No, see he's got 'Empty Liverpool' when, um, the ship's sunk down a bit. But that's a colder country. That should be the other way round, that's why it should be the other way round.
Mark: What, so 'Liverpool' should be there and the 'Foreign' one should be there?
Michelle: Yeah.
Teacher: Why is that?
Michelle: Well, because um, we've said that Liverpool's cold, coldest in the winter, and um, the sea's more dense and so the ship can float more in that.
Teacher: It floats higher does it?
Michelle: Yeah, it floats higher than in a 'Foreign country', 'cos that's hot. And you've (to Mark) put the 'Foreign country', say, instead of 'Liverpool', because the boat in Liverpool floats higher than in the foreign country. But you've put it the other way round.

Mark was able to redraw his Plimsoll line correctly by himself. Michelle's explanation helped him to do so.

Role-play promotes the social aspects of science

Science has a social and moral aspect in addition to its analytical and problem-solving facets. Producing a group product about science, in the form of a TV commercial, documentary, or radio news item is a valuable way of helping children to weigh evidence, make value judgements and confirm their understanding.

A class of seven- to eight-year-olds debated the controversial issue of the coming of a new link road to their town (Carré 1987). Data collection and interviews with local people culminated in a 'public enquiry' where the children, in different roles, presented their case in front of television cameras. Four groups represented 'Conservationists', 'Chamber of Trade and Commerce', 'Residents' and 'Town Planners.' The children worked for weeks to prepare their case. The aim was to get them to make rational, informed and

solve, as follows. A ship sailing from Liverpool to Bombay in January is thought to be carrying far too much cargo. Can they bring the wicked captain to justice by devising a way to show that his ship is overloaded? The children designed their own 'watermarks' (Plimsoll lines) for their imaginary ships (which one child immediately identified as the equivalent of their straw hydrometers). The teacher wanted them to understand that different densities of sea-water affect floating objects in different ways. The children produced a variety of Plimsoll lines, all of which were slightly incorrect in some way. However, all of them, apart from Mark, understood that the highest mark on a ship's waterline would represent a loaded ship in a hot climatic region, in less dense sea-water.

Teacher: Look at Mark's again there. The lowest line on his water-line is a 'Foreign independent choices, and develop a concern for others. Here are some statements made during their group sessions practising for interviewing adults in town, and during interviews.

- Don't you care about people, only about trees? (a role playing member of the traders meeting the conservationists' group).
- Can't you see any good in it, Mr X? (Child's question to an adult of a local preservation society when he appeared to be totally biased.)
- Would you like to live in one of the new houses? (Child's forthright question to an estate agent who favoured the scheme.)
- ('Resident' to 'town planner'): How is this going to make Exmouth a better holiday resort?
- ('Planner's' reply, almost certainly gleaned from meeting a real developer, but aptly reproduced): Because you wouldn't have things like the new swimming pool if there aren't enough people living here to pay for it. Budleigh hasn't got a swimming pool, has it, 'cos it's too small.

By the time of the Inquiry some children had developed sufficient insights for the emergence of genuine autonomous viewpoints to emerge, as for example when a girl suddenly detached herself from the role-play and spoke from the heart. 'I'm against it - I really am ...'

The importance of giving children opportunities to become conscious of controlling and directing their own thinking cannot be underestimated. Margaret Donaldson (1978), says that 'we heighten our awareness of what is actual by considering what is possible. We are conscious also of what we do not do - of what we might have done. The notion of choice is thus central'. Some children in this class did choose to direct their thinking, holding on to their own viewpoint after consideration of alternative ways of thinking, a condition implicit in any idea of intellectual and moral autonomy.

This is particularly important to encourage, for science is not restricted to laboratory-type events. It is important that primary children can discuss science in a

broad context. Science awareness needs to be encouraged in life generally.

Talking about science in the news

Encouraging discussion about topical issues is a good way of developing children's talk. One teacher has a small notice board in her room with a heading 'Don't Snooze through News'. Newspaper items, and other texts, are intended to inform and provoke. The seven-year-olds are encouraged to talk to their parents about current science news items, and to argue for and against the issues. On the board recently I saw news clippings about 'pesticides', 'pollution' and the 'power of the Green Consumer'. Morning news-time is about their views of the world, gleaned from TV, newspapers, junk mail and the like.

Is there science in other subjects?

Another teacher encouraged her ten-year-olds to collect information about the Greenhouse Effect, the phenomenon by which much of the sun's radiant heat is reflected back into space, but a portion is absorbed and retained within our atmosphere. What do young children understand about this concept?

Pupil 1: Well, the Greenhouse Effect is a global problem and it's breaking up the ozone layer which is letting through the sun's strong rays. The ozone layer is what filters the powerful rays of the sun which stops us from being damaged.
Pupil 2: The people using methane and gas, fossil fuels and aerosols cause the damage by letting the gases...and that...into the air.

Although their language mimics that of their teacher and of news items, their talk is not empty verbalisation. As Joanne explained,'''Global'' means that it affects the whole earth. ''Filter'' means that so much of a substance is absorbed and the

Work on the Bayeux Tapestry enabled children to be sceptical when handling evidence.

rest goes straight through'. Jane said of her phrase, 'letting gases into the air', that 'the gases hold the heat in the atmosphere'.

Perhaps their degree of understanding of a complex idea is encouraged by a teacher who respects what the children have to offer and gives them opportunities to express their ideas.

Although some primary schools will teach science as isolated lessons, the National Curriculum does not prescribe methods; teachers can be flexible. Science as part of a cross-curricular approach is relatively common, but it is not all that common to find a teacher who plans thematic work with process skills in mind.

As the climax to a term's work on Norman history, a class assembly explained to the school how historians believe King Harold met his death. Their own copy of the Bayeux Tapestry was used so that children had a chance to talk about this secondary source of evidence.

Pupil 1: This picture is the only clue we have from the Norman times, and the arrow may not have gone in his eye and may not have hit him. The chances are that many more men could have been wounded with an injury to the eye!

Pupil 2: We don't know who Harold is on this tapestry. He might be another figure like this man falling to the ground. The title of 'Harold' is over more than one person.

Pupil 3: This weaving was done in about 1080, about twenty years after the Battle of Hastings. All of us know we can't remember things exactly and we forget what happens. These weavers would have needed perfect memories after 20 years. And they weren't even there, for they were women.

The drama of simulated battle and the discussions which ensued helped the class

119

to be sceptical when handling evidence, to sort fact from opinion and to engage in argument. These are sophisticated tasks for nine-year-olds, but thinking processes in science are not widely different from the way we think in history, or in everyday life.

Learning about planning experiments through purposeful play

Science is as much about processes as it is about products. An initial stage in planning an experiment is to identify those variables that need to be changed, those that need to be measured and those that need to be kept the same for a fair test. To build upon a class of six-year olds' existing understanding of the concept of 'fairness', an experiment to try to find out 'who is the best ball bouncer?' was developed. The independent variable was the child, the

dependent variable was the height to which the ball bounced. For a fair test the nature of the floor, the type of ball, the size of ball, the force applied to the ball and so on needed to be constrained. There was little doubt about the latter list, provoked by the teacher's continual cheating! For example, the teacher used a 'super ball' and the children used a punctured football:

Pupil: That one bounces small.
Teacher: Oh it has? The would mean - what are you telling me then? If it's got to be fair - a fair game ...
Pupil: You have to have the same ball.

Other examples of 'cheating' included getting the children to bounce their ball on the thick mat while the teacher used the hard floor, and measuring inaccurately the children's bounces.

The children sorted out most of the rules about 'being fair' and made an excellent suggestion to cope with the different types of ball being used.

Teacher: So there's three things you're telling me then aren't you? You're saying ... hey ... it's not fair ... I'm bigger than Andrea.

An experiment to find out who is the best ball bouncer.

We should really be the same size ... you're telling me that um ... I hit it harder than Andrew and that's not fair because we've both got to push it down as hard as each other ... and the third thing you said?
Pupil: The ball was softer than yours.
Teacher: That the ball was softer than mine? So really we should to be fair. How can we cope with that if we need to be fair, what can we do?
Pupil: You could take it in turns with the ball?
Teacher: That's a wonderful suggestion isn't it? Now, if we take it in turns we would use the same ball wouldn't we?

At the very end of the afternoon one of the children in the class suggested, 'If we're going to be really fair all these must be done at the same time.' By 'all these' she meant 'all the ball bouncing'. Her concern for simultaneous performances was commendable. We couldn't conceive of such a refinement in real life. Children probably never realize how clever their insights are!

It is impossible to make a sensible statement about learning science without the proviso that one learns about it in a particular way. The learning that goes on is governed by the context provided by the teacher. A teacher's assumptions about the nature of science, about school science activity and about the use of language within the class will all influence the sort of learning that goes on. The examples given in this chapter may challenge you to check your personal beliefs about these three components, particularly if you perceive talk to be a catalyst in changing ideas.

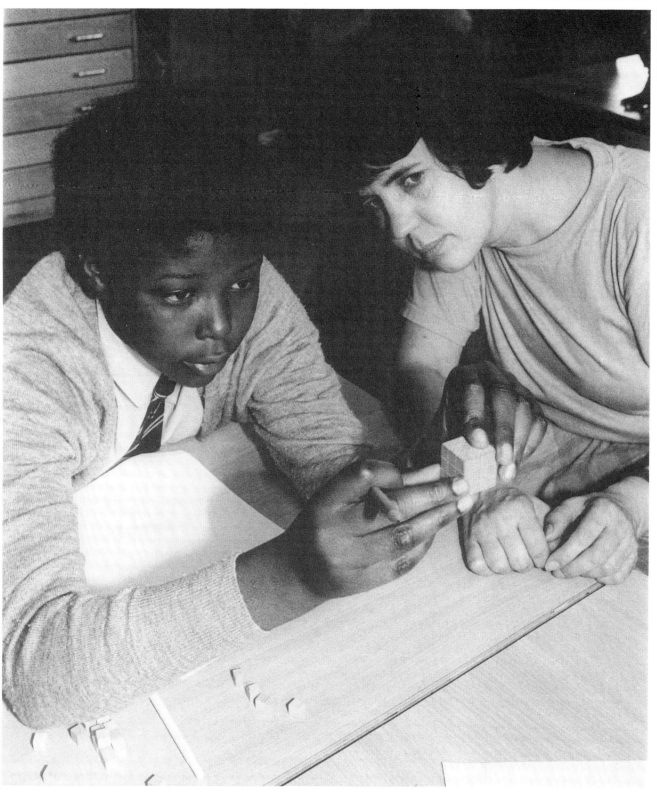

Talk in mathematics
Janet Duffin

Talk in mathematics
Janet Duffin

INTRODUCTION

'Traditionally mathematics time in the primary school has been the quiet time of the day; now it's often the noisiest because the children all have something to say to each other about the mathematics they are doing.'

This seems to be the best reason for mathematics talk, or indeed any talk: that the speaker has something they want to say to somebody else about something that is important to them. But it is not the only reason for developing talk in the mathematics classroom today.

Other reasons are:
- New realisations about the ways in which talk can help children to learn, so that teachers can understand where their children's learning is at any particular time.
- Changes in the real world which are bringing new resources into the classroom and creating new responsibilities for teachers, who need to be able to maximise the potential of these resources.
- Changes in the skills appropriate to a changed world, making some less relevant than they used to be while making others more important

Mathematics and language

Teachers have long realised that children have to be able to associate the special symbols of mathematics with words in ordinary, everyday language. Many have worked hard at helping children to make these associations by, for example, relating addition (+) to phrases like: 'is more than', 'add', 'plus', 'increase by' etc and the other three basic symbols (-, x, ÷) to similarly appropriate forms of words. Unfortunately, these efforts have not always been associated with talk in the classroom. They have tended instead to concentrate on matching words and phrases to the appropriate symbols.

Moreover, some other, less useful forms of words have also traditionally been associated with the basic arithmetical operations. Terms like 'borrow', phrases like 'five from two you can't' and 'turn it upside down and multiply' have been introduced by teachers almost worldwide to try to help children to carry out complicated procedures on paper. These have not always been successful in achieving their purpose. Indeed in some cases they have impeded progress, created confusion and provided a source of later difficulty.

It is now becoming clear that one of the main reasons for the problems often encountered is that these phrases and forms of words were largely decided upon by the teacher rather than arising naturally from children's activities. They came from the teacher's perception of mathematics and from the teacher's language rather than the children's. The realisation that children's own language can be used to extend their understanding is fairly new in mathematics.

How children's thinking can be highlighted through talk

In a classroom recently the teacher had been talking with the children about how it was possible sometimes to make a subtraction easier than it seemed to be on first sight. They had been thinking about the best way of taking 199 or 201 from another number, 357, for example. The teacher suggested that perhaps it might make the subtraction easier to do if they were to think of a different number to subtract first. They supplied 200 as an easier number to subtract and then decided what to do in each of the two cases of subtracting 199 and 201 instead. They tried some examples.

A child in one of the groups seemed to be having some difficulty. He had tried to make what had come out of the talk into a rule for himself, and was subtracting one more for 199 and adding one on for 201. The teacher was trying to help by looking at it

from a commonsense point of view but he seemed unable to understand. Another child in the group suddenly said 'Perhaps he's thinking about it in a different way from you and that's why he can't understand what you are saying.' This serves to highlight the fact that it is very important for teachers to be sensitive to children's thinking. Another important point to remember is that teachers learn from talk as well as children. The above incident illustrates this well.

On another occasion some children were 'making 100' and their teacher had suggested, after they had produced 90 and 10, 80 and 20 etc, that they might like to look for some numbers without zeros which would also make 100. One boy offering 53 and 47 explained it as follows: 'Well, I know that 50 and 50 make a 100 and so if I have some figures in the units it will come to more than 100, so I put 50 and 40 because that makes 90. Then I said that three and seven make ten so I made it 53 and 47'.

This is clearly a child who has been encouraged to talk in mathematics and has become very able at describing the mathematics he has done. But his way was again not the teacher's, which was 'I know

Children learn from talking and discussing in mathematics.

50 and 50 make 100 so I add three on to one of the 50s and then I have to take away three from the other. That gives me 53 and 47 to make 100.' He listened carefully to the teacher's way but decided that he preferred his own. This time the teacher had shared her method with the child without forcing it upon him.

This example shows:

• a child who is able to explain and justify his mathematics,
• a child who is prepared to listen to another's way of doing some mathematics before deciding that he prefers his own method,
• that, by listening to them, a teacher can find out far more about how children are thinking and where they are than is possible from written exercises alone.

Of course, not all children can articulate their mathematics as well and clearly as this boy could, but the example shows what can be achieved when children are used to being asked to explain and talk about their thinking. However, this does not come about without considerable effort. Both teachers and children have to learn how to operate in this way.

Most teachers already realise the importance of talk as an integral part of early language development. Indeed they increasingly see its effectiveness in many other areas of the primary curriculum. They need to take it on board as an element in mathematics too, and to realise that mathematics can often enrich talk in other areas of the curriculum.

Talk, creative writing and mathematics

Most primary teachers would not find unusual the idea that it is important to talk before attempting creative writing, for example. When teachers become aware of the mathematics everywhere around them, it too can be brought into creative writing.

For example, a teacher taking a class which was doing some creative writing about cops and robbers said she didn't think there would be any mathematics in that. However, after the class had a discussion on symmetry they thought there might be things which could have happened to the robbers to make them asymmetrical so that they could be identified by cops who might be chasing them. The ideas they had were amazing, and their teacher said they later produced some wonderful writing - bringing in mathematics!

So mathematical ideas can feed talk in other subject areas. Indeed, there was an experiment carried out in the Netherlands, designed to bring talk into mathematics lessons with the idea of improving performance in mathematics, which succeeded, as was shown in subsequent testing of the children, in improving their language performance as much as it improved their mathematics, if not more.

Mathematics can be brought into most creative writing.

Talking for reading mathematics

Just as teachers will find that talking through ideas can help children to see how to write about what they have done, they will also find it helps them to read mathematics.

All teachers realise that speech is associated with children's ability to read: that those children who come to school with little speech are unlikely to find reading easy and that all children read most easily words which are already part of their spoken vocabulary. A lack of practice in talking about mathematics can also impede children's ability to read mathematics textbooks.

The formal language associated with mathematics includes words and phrases which do not form part of the ordinary speech of everyday life. However, in reading mathematics, and in reading about it, it is essential to have a ready understanding of these words and phrases. Mathematics talk in the classroom, developed to enable pupils to communicate and explain the mathematics they are doing, could well also help them to read mathematics, and about mathematics.

The new technology as a classroom resource

Calculators and computers now feature widely in the everyday life of most people in the community; they are also rapidly becoming accepted pieces of equipment in many classrooms. It is most important that they should be used to their maximum potential.

This requires us to recognise that they not only make some traditional techniques and skills less useful (some would say redundant), but they also introduce a need for children to acquire a new set of skills related to computer and calculator use. It has been said that, while this new technology takes away the need for the complex calculations that were a major part of a school's mathematics diet before its arrival, it makes the ability to explain and justify mathematical processes more important than before. The new technology also requires understanding of the processes involved in using it. This understanding can best be judged through talk with children.

Explanation and justification, therefore, take on a new importance. So, with the emphasis on heavy calculation reduced, how do we begin to help children to be able to explain and justify their mathematics so that they can be better equipped for the world they will enter after school?

An important way to achieve this is through talk, through sharing mathematics, through working and talking together instead of doing mathematics in isolation with few opportunities for anything other than recording it in its own specific symbolic forms.

Talk with the children about using new technology such as calculators is essential.

Talk and the National Curriculum

Ben Carter

The National Curriculum reinforces the importance of talk by requiring pupils to be able to:

- work collaboratively in mathematics,
- interpret information from a graph, a calculator or a computer,
- explain and justify mathematical results obtained.

If these aims are to be achieved then the ability to talk about and share mathematics, as well as the ability to explain, interpret and justify must be developed from an early age.

Learning to listen

Both children and teachers need to learn to listen; children to listen to each other and to their teacher, and teachers to listen to their children. This is not as easy as it may sound, partly because certain conventions about classroom questioning and answering have developed in schools, and these can inhibit both teachers and children. How often, in mathematics lessons, do questions appear to make children freeze? How can we change the climate from one in which the teacher's questions inhibit talk to one in which they draw out children's thinking? Learning to listen to the answers is an important part of this.

Teachers learning to listen

Some teachers have to make quite a radical change in their teaching style in order to become good at listening to what children say. Most teachers have developed with experience a competent 'question and answer' technique designed to enable them to question children in order to elicit a specific answer or to enable them, by questioning, to lead children through a thinking process. Although these still have a place in the classroom, teachers also need to develop a new 'listening' way of questioning which is radically different from either of these two well-established methods of using questions.

The difference is that, instead of the teacher questioning for a specific answer or a specific thinking strategy, he or she is now questioning without an expected answer in mind. It is the child's response which is important and this response may well show a different way of thinking from that of the teacher.

That is to say that the teacher has to realise that the child may answer in a way which is totally unexpected, and there is a need to be able to accept this without feeling threatened or being threatening. Several new elements now enter into the process of questioning and interchange between teacher and child. These include:

• allowing the child plenty of thinking time for articulating an appropriate answer,
• not turning to another child if the one questioned seems to be having difficulty,
• being able to offer encouraging interjections and avoid making the child feel hassled by providing the thinking time he or she may need.

The vital thing to be aware of in attempting to work with children in this way is that the outcome is meant to be about the child's thinking rather than the teacher's. This is easier to say than to carry out.

Teachers trying it for the first time speak of the difficulty they have in refraining from intervening in order to help the child see how to proceed. Their anxiety arises from their care for the children, which in itself can make listening without intervening more difficult. However, once this is accepted, teachers are genuinely amazed at the difference it makes to their lessons.

They begin to say that they now know what is going on in there (tapping their heads); that their old method of operating failed to make them aware of how their children were progresssing, let alone how they were thinking.

Teachers who have accepted this new way of working say they would never dream of returning to the way they taught before. They claim that now they know more about their children's ways of thinking, this knowledge enables them to be much more

Teachers need to learn to listen as well as the children.

efficient in selecting suitable activities. In some cases they are amazed to discover that their view of their children's progress has been transformed. Because of new insights into the working of children's minds, they say that they now see quite differently the children they thought were not very good at mathematics.

With this new method, the teacher's view of children's progress is geared much more to what the children are able to explain and how well they can justify their ideas and methods. In fact, they find that their evaluation of the children's work begins to match much more closely the new requirements mentioned earlier, in relation both to the National Curriculum and to new expectations created by the arrival of calculators and computers.

Children learning to listen

It is very easy for children to get excited about a piece of mathematics they have been doing, and to fail to listen to what others are saying to them. The following example illustrates this well.

Some children were using the plan of a house they had made to explain about the area of the ground it covered. They had already found out how to calculate the area of simple rectangular shapes but they now had to try to see how to adapt this to more complex shapes.

Two of them were arguing vehemently about how to do it; neither was listening to the other, both were sure they knew the way. One had shouted out the final answer, the other was trying, rather hesitantly, to explain the steps of the calculation. In fact their methods were very similar, but they had no time to listen to each other and the picture presented was one of discord and disagreement.

Their teacher said they were always vying with each other, and that one was very quick but had a tendency to be careless in calculation, while the other was more careful. One had good visual perception and could arrive at an answer intuitively, while the other looked first for a strategy for calculating. Both could explain their ideas when asked but they were not yet working collaboratively. In order to communicate

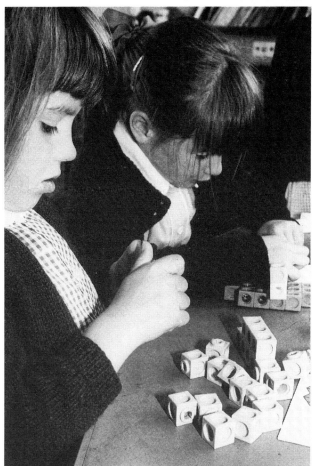

Children need to listen to each other when working together.

effectively, and eventually to benefit from each other's natural way of working as well, it was essential that they learn to listen.

One way I have seen of encouraging children to listen to each other is to put their names on a sheet in the classroom, and put colour-coded marks opposite each name indicating 'explains well', 'needs to get better at explaining', 'listens well', 'needs to get better at listening'. Both teacher and children can fill in this chart. At a glance both children and teacher can see how the children are measuring up in these skills; at a glance the teacher can see which children have not done much explaining and have not been listened to very much. In this way he or she has an immediate check on the children's progress and can try to ensure that an opportunity is found for those with little or nothing opposite their names to be listened to specifically in the coming days. There must be time for listening and talking in every classroom.

Organising for talk

Many teachers who want to develop this kind of talk in their mathematics lessons find it very difficult to organise. They speak of the difficulty when all the children are clamouring for attention, and of the problem of having a big class so that they cannot get round to talk with all their children.

Some suggestions for attempting to organise the classroom for talk are given here:

- Encourage children to work together, in pairs or in small groups.
- Make sure that the activities you plan for them are easily done in pairs or small groups.
- Use games to encourage talk. Make sure that children are accustomed to the conventions of games playing: taking turns, waiting for each to finish his or her turn before proceeding. Mayhem can be caused in a classroom by children who have never learned these rules.

- Remember that project work and cross-curricular activities also offer opportunities for appropriate mathematical talk.
- Make it part of your normal classroom practice to work with a small group of children when you want to develop a specific skill or discuss a specific thinking strategy with them. Remember that you will need to see that the rest of the class is gainfully employed on activities that will not demand too much of your attention for the moment.
- Have a fund of resource material easily accessible around the room so that children do not need to come and ask your permission to get it. A little time spent on training them to use equipment sensibly is well worth the effort. It will free you from having to supervise all use of material and equipment, giving you more time for talk with individuals and groups of children. One teacher I know undertook a complete reorganisation of her classroom with the help of the children so that after that, the children knew where everything was and

Games are a good way to organise the classroom for talk.

felt that the classroom equipment was theirs to be used for the benefit of them all.

• Most primary classrooms are organised with an area for talk and sharing experiences and news. Use this to encourage the children to talk about and share the mathematics they may have been doing. A few minutes of this each day can help to build up the habit of talking about mathematics.

• One idea I have seen is to set up a 'recording room' where the children can go to record on tape a piece of mathematics they may want to tell the teacher about, when he or she is too busy to listen to them. This of course brings in another piece of modern equipment which will increasingly be used in classrooms. As with most other pieces of classroom equipment, children have to learn how to use the tape recorder sensibly. Initially their attempts will not be very successful, but they can learn to use it properly, given patience and the right classroom environment.

The teacher's role in a 'talking' classroom

All the ideas mentioned so far depend upon teachers being able to adjust their thinking, their classroom style and the way in which they view their relationship with children, if these do not already fit in with the suggestions made.

Through classroom talk, the teacher's role becomes subtly different from the traditional view of it. If children are to be listened to, then what they have to say must be valued and accepted. The teacher must no longer be seen as the person in the classroom who knows everything, with the children there to take in without question what he or she has to offer.

Many teachers have changed their role in accordance with these ideas, but for some it may be quite difficult to encompass. The normal pattern of teacher-pupil interchange in the classroom has been described as the 'three term sequence'. The teacher asks a question - the child gives an answer - the teacher judges the answer. Implicit in this

Recording information for a busy teacher to listen to later on is very effective.

convention is the idea that the teacher always knows the answer to any question asked and is seeking to know whether the child can also supply it.

This method of discourse cannot advance mathematics talk in the ways advocated in this chapter. Discussion between teacher and children has to resemble more the talk between equals, when questions are asked because the questioner does not know the answer and wants to find out. This change can be quite difficult to adjust to, and teachers find it difficult at first to refrain from intervening. They often say things like 'I'm itching to tell them but I know I mustn't' as they describe their initial attempts.

One of the most crucial features of this perception of classroom talk is learning to accept that what a child says is a demonstration of where his or her thinking stands, rather than seeing it as 'wrong' because it does not match the teacher's expectations. Listening, in this context, includes not forcing the teacher's perception on the child.

Children sometimes find it very difficult at first to explain how they have arrived at an answer, but this becomes easier with practice. At first they may appear to be tongue-tied when asked to explain. Their first attempts will be to say things like 'I just knew it' or 'I just did it in my brain'.

Later they may begin to say things like 'I got the answer to the first bit and then I put it in the back of my brain and counted the rest in the front of my brain.' This articulate description shows a high level of command of language but it is not yet describing aptly the actual thought processes. This comes even later, when children are becoming more accustomed to the idea of explaining their mathematics.

Children often need time to explain how they arrived at an answer.

Here are some explanations given by children who are becoming able to talk about mathematics in a way approaching what is to be required of them in the National Curriculum.

- Explaining how to find two times ninety nine: 'Well, two times a hundred is two hundred and ninety nine is one less than a hundred so two ninety nines will be a hundred and ninety eight.'
- Explaining how the answer of 13 was arrived at for six and seven added together: 'Well, I know that two sixes is twelve, so it must be one more than that.'
- Explaining an activity designed to help children to understand about odd and even numbers: 'Well, I'm sorting them out into sets of two, and if there is one left over I know it's an odd number, but if there are none left over I know it's even.'
- Talking about scoring in a game: 'You get two every time you are right, and you lose two points every time you get it wrong. I'm at -14 now, but if I get it right the next time I'll get up to -12, and if I go on getting it right I'll get back to the plus numbers.'

Sometimes children ask their teacher a question and, on being asked to explain a bit more about the problem, they may realise the answer to the question without being told it. Sometimes too, when explaining an answer, children will realise they have made a mistake in their working and will correct it on the spot. How much better than going to do their corrections after getting the teacher's 'cross' on their book! It can also be helpful to children to ask them to read back to you what they have written down; this way they get used to looking at what they have done and become less likely to accept a ridiculous answer without question.

A final word

While in the process of trying to effect changes in their classroom which will give a high priority to talk, teachers will find it beneficial to talk about mathematics amongst themselves. The days set aside for school in-service work are excellent for this kind of activity. Try to set aside some time for teachers to try out mathematical activities suitable for their children and encourage them to talk about their answers to these, their ways of arriving at their answers, and their justification of them.

Reflection about the outcome of these discussions can lead to insights into the value of mathematics talk which can then be used to help develop it in the classroom.

Awareness of language
Sarah Tann

Awareness of language
Sarah Tann

INTRODUCTION

The HMI document 'English 5-16 Curriculum Matters No 1' (1985) argued that children needed 'knowledge about language'. This was an unfamiliar phrase, and led to heated debate about its meaning and implications. In the subsequent Kingman Report (1988a) this phrase came to be equated with a model of language comprised of four elements: knowledge about the forms and functions of language; about communication and comprehension; about the acquisition of language; and about its geographical and historical variations.

Kingman suggested that 'successful communication depends upon a recognition and accurate use of the rules and conventions' of language, but urged that there should not be 'a return to old-fashioned grammar teaching' (para 1.11). It suggested that helping pupils is a 'subtle process which requires the teacher to intervene constructively and at an appropriate time' (para 2.28). This should happen 'mainly through exploration of the language the pupils use rather than through exercises out of context ... so that explicit statement consolidates the implicit understanding' (para 2.30) which is helpful to the development of their language ability. So teaching about language should not be 'bolted on' (para 4.53). This approach is confirmed in the second Cox Report (1989).

The Kingman Report mentioned the importance of talk as a mode of communication and a tool for learning and therefore the need to develop it effectively. Also, an 'awareness' of British regional differences in vocabulary and accent, as well as an awareness of other languages, is considered important so that children develop a 'civilised respect' for other languages (para 4.33). The Report goes on to identify some different kinds of talk in terms of different purposes. For example, teachers need to encourage talk 'which can be exploratory, tentative, used for thinking through problems, for discussing assigned tasks, and for clarifying thought ... also to present an argument rationally and logically' (para 4.34).

Apart from the purposes for which talk can be used, and the importance of learning to analyse its appropriateness and effectiveness, Kingman states that there are other aspects of oral language which are of importance and interest to children. For example, 'children are fascinated by word games - by puns, backslang, tongue-twisters, conundrums, anagrams, palindromes, etymologies and 'secret' languages ...' (para 2.29, and also mentioned in the Programmes of study for Key Stage 1, Attainment Target 3, and Attainment Target 2, level 5 DES 1989). Also, children will be helped, Kingman says, by having a 'descriptive technical language' through which they can discuss language. Kingman suggests that awareness of the forms of language is an entirely natural development which the teacher can encourage and through which children can acquire this technical language, for 'language is a naming experience, and what we name we have power over' (para 1.1).

However, in the context of oracy, what does knowledge about language mean? What kinds of knowledge about oral language should we try to make explicit? Are we to talk about the process of talking, how we learn to talk, and about the kinds of words and expressions we use when talking? Are we also to focus on 'oral traditions'? How are we to talk about talking, listening, and understanding? By

what means should we demonstrate this explicit knowledge? If we are to make such knowledge explicit, do we need a specialist vocabulary with which to discuss oracy - a metalanguage, or language with which to discuss language? What aspects of oracy can we expect primary children to discuss and what metalanguage do they need? Finally, how certain are we that explicit knowledge about language does in fact improve our understanding, our use, or our pleasure in language?

The subsequent Cox Reports (DES 1988b, 1989) suggested a number of oracy skills which primary children should acquire (English Attainment Target 1), including listening to instructions, listening and responding to books, participating in discussions, describing events and giving presentations, using transactional language and, at Level 5, showing awareness of regional differences in vocabulary. The programmes of study suggest that children should 'reflect upon and evaluate their use of spoken language and reformulate it to

It is important that children develop a 'civilised respect' for other languages.

help the listener', and adjust the language they use and its delivery 'to suit particular audiences, purposes and contexts' (15.27). More oral skills are included in the Reading Attainment Target, where children should be encouraged to talk about books, and in the Writing Attainment Target, where children should be also encouraged to talk about their own writing and other people's. Furthermore, oracy has been given equal weight with reading and writing in terms of assessment.

Apart from the English curriculum, in the other core curriculum areas there are also frequent references to children's need to describe, explain, check, review and report on their mathematical and scientific activities. 'Communication' as a cross-curricular skill exists in its own right in the National Curriculum. Clearly the status of oral language is rising.

However, in addition to increasing children's awareness of oral language processes, purposes and contexts, Cox (DES 1989) also suggested that although teachers should introduce knowledge about the nature and functions of language in Standard English in 'the top years of the primary school' (6.3), in general there is no obligation concerning formal 'knowledge about language' till Level 5. Although these features may well be talked about, they are situated in the writing component. For example, in the programmes of study, Attainment Target 3, key stage 1, it is suggested that children could be introduced, through the context of their own writing, to such terms as 'sentence', 'verb', 'tense', 'noun' and 'pronoun'. Only at Key Stage 2 is any mention made in the Attainment Targets of knowledge of such things as the wider range of sentence connectives; then at Level 3, punctuation devices are brought in, and sentence structures at Level 4, including subordinate clauses , with word structures such as prefixes, suffixes and inflectional endings at Level 5.

However, interest in oral language and 'knowledge about language' is not new. The kinds of formal 'knowledge about language' mentioned in the Kingman and Cox Reports have for a long time been part of the wider 'language awareness' movement. This movement has for some time urged that a more general sensitivity to language could help to end the parochial view of language which seems so dominant in this country. The aims are both cognitive and affective: to reveal the richness of language variety and to increase knowledge of the patterns, nature, structure, systems and rules of language; to strengthen study skills in learning languages; to encourage children to realise the value of language in human life and the centrality of communication to healthy development; to arouse curiosity concerning the diversity within our language environment and heritage, and to celebrate the diversity of language and the pleasures this discovery can bring. In trying to achieve such ends it is important to use the children as the main resource because their language is so rich and relevant to themselves. It is also important to encourage them to see that their own languages are a valued resource.

More oral skills have been included in the Reading and Writing Attainment Targets.

Playground talk (rhymes, riddles, and rib-ticklers), nicknames, TV generated contemporary phrases, 'in talk' and 'out talk', regional differences, generational differences: the children are the experts and the final arbitrators on meanings and significances in all such matters that concern 'their' language.

Within this broader background to both the recent Reports two distinct reasons for developing knowledge about language can be discerned:

- It is instrumental: heightening awareness of oral skills and strategies can improve their understanding and use,
- It is interesting: the study of language, its patterns and varieties is of interest and value and is an entitlement for all children.

Instrumental knowledge about oral language

Talking about discussion strategies and skills

Interactive group discussions are situations which many teachers avoid (Galton, Simon and Croll 1980). They are often believed to be problematic for three main reasons. It can be difficult to motivate children if talk is t already established as a valuable mode of learning. Group work is also sometimes thought to be difficult to manage in a busy classroom, and in particular, it can be difficult to monitor.

However, children can and do learn through group discussions. They are also aware of some difficulties which they can experience in group discussion sessions. These relate both to the nature of the tasks set and to the composition of the groups.

For example, a junior class was quick to point out that being asked to discuss something (a poem, or some current event or issue featured on *Newsround*) without prior warning and preparation usually ended with banal results or in an argument. The children found these tasks 'unreal' and felt it was only worth discussing something if it ended up with a decision and some 'real action'. They also made pertinent comments about the size and mix of the groups, the personalities, gender and abilities, and they distinguished between people they like to sit with and people that they like to work with - because 'You sometimes muck about with your friends. It's best to choose to work with someone sensible'.

The children were also very articulate in drawing distinctions between discussions and arguments (quarrels), and could identify a number of useful strategies for preventing the one becoming the other. The differences between these two situations were readily identified in terms of both goals (purposes) and listener responses (process strategies). Starting from an analysis of recent TV 'soap' episodes (there are always arguments in soaps) the children were able to identify specific examples of positive and negative strategies and were also able to suggest remedial action to change either the outcome or the feelings generated.

Differences between discussions and arguments were quickly listed, and terminology generated to describe the language functions, process strategies and skills as perceived by the children. 'In a discussion you try to come to an agreement', 'you try to find out what the others think' (goals), so, 'you've got to be willing to try to understand what the other person means', 'you've got to be ready to give your own opinion, details, reasons, make comparisons', 'you've got to know how to chip in', 'you've got to show you are listening by your expression', (processes). 'If it starts to turn into an argument, you've got to try to calm them, agree with them a bit, listen to them, get them to explain it again, ask them to say it differently, ask more questions, bribe them, get them drunk...'. These ideas (mostly) show a mature understanding of the social demands made of a listener, and why good discussions are so hard to achieve!

In another school, children in the infant class found it easy to demonstrate different kinds of talk, for different purposes, and to different audiences. Any adult eavesdropping in the 'home corner', 'shop', or 'doctor's surgery' will soon be convinced of the children's implicit knowledge of how language is used by different people to different effects. Listening to playground

Playground talk is an excellent example of how children can use language to manipulate others.

talk also offers an impressive display of how adept some children can be at using language to manipulate others and to get what they want.

At this early age it is often difficult for children to talk about what they understand, but they can easily give you examples to illustrate their implicit grasp of non-verbal and paraverbal features. Children will, for example, show how they use their voices differently, and identify para-verbal variables in terms of their affective functions, for example, 'talk posh, all la-di-da', 'talk very kindly', 'talk bossily'. They will also explain that they talk differently to different people and demonstrate how they vary vocabulary, register and style, for example, 'I'm not allowed to swear at my Mum', 'When we talk with our friends we can use naughty words', 'You mustn't just say "yes" or "no" to the Head or he'll say its rude'.

Developing awareness of discussion skills

Reception and infant children on entering school can and do already talk purposefully and confidently to a variety of people, in groups of different sizes, for different reasons and in different ways. Although many children arrive at school as skilled communicators (Tizard and Hughes 1984, Wells 1987) others clearly do not - in English or any other language. But with a clear school policy and sufficient time invested in talk, in talking about talk, and in using it to learn about things which are important to the children, the whole class can begin to become effective talkers during their first year and begin to be explicit about the necessary strategies and skills.

How can children become good talkers? How can a teacher help children to develop as talkers? What are we aiming for? How can we monitor their progress?

From the start, discussion has to figure prominently. However, it takes time to develop a class of talkers. For example, a whole class could meet together three or four times a day for periods of about 20 minutes each. First thing in the morning, at register time, there is a chance for anyone to tell the others some important news that they just must get off their chest. The important skill here, for the speaker, is to remember that the rest of the class doesn't know the problems that you might have been having with your baby brother and why last night was so exciting. So the speaker has to learn to start before the 'beginning', to give the background before the event last night. The listeners have to learn to listen and follow the story, and to try to understand why it is so important to the speaker. They have to get inside the speaker's shoes to appreciate the story fully and make sympathetic and supportive comments.

During an exchange of news the children initially need to be reminded of the Golden Rules, for example:

Discussions have to play an important role in the classroom for children to become effective 'talkers and listeners'.

- Don't all talk together,
- Don't interrupt anyone,
- Listen to the person who is speaking.

At first the teacher may field the contributions and direct the discussion. She may call on the children who are 'bidding' for their turn - usually by putting up their hand. To encourage listening, the teacher needs to ask another child to comment on what a speaker has said: 'What do you think?', 'What would you have done?' or 'Something like that happened to you the other day, didn't it?'. To encourage the children to clarify or extend their contributions, she may ask further specific questions (for clarification) or general open ones (to encourage further reflection, elaboration or exploration of ideas). Finally, she can indicate that she values their views and news by listening to them herself and by creating opportunities for the rest of the class to listen also. It is also helpful to identify the particular skill demonstrated, to label and reinforce it, thus helping children to recognise it in practice ('You *explained* that beautifully', 'That's a very good *reason*'). The contribution can also be rewarded by praise indicated by tone of voice and expression ('That's a marvellous *idea*').

Another aspect of a classroom of talkers is that there might always be a project on the go, one to which every child can contribute because every child is participating in a common area of investigation. An important feature of such a way of working is to let the children take greater responsibility for the planning and decision-making processes. It takes longer this way. There is less, immediately, to show for it, and less to put up on the wall, but it allows the children to do all the real thinking and talking 'for real'. It has practical outcomes upon which the children can take action, and with that opportunity comes all the interest, involvement and motivation.

For example, an infant class which was working on 'sight' had, amongst other things, explored a model of an eye (and looked at their own eyes) and discussed how we see. They had reflected on what it was like to be blind. They had done experiments to find out how well they could see in the distance or in the dark, and to find their angle of vision, ie how far to each side they can see. They had imagined what it would be like to have eyes in the back of their head. They also had worked with mirrors. Now they were going into town to the new shopping complex which had lots of distorting glass. The children planned the trip. They knew they would be going in a mini-bus, but they had to decide how many would fit in, how much it would cost, which route to choose, how long it would take, what equipment they would need, and what to have for lunch.

The children eventually dispersed to find maps and bus company addresses, and to ask everyone in the class what they wanted on the picnic. The result of these investigations was a sketch map of the chosen route, and the measured distance in string and miles. There was a picture of the bus filling up with a specified number of gallons and the total cost of the fuel indicated. Finally, there was a bar chart

A visit to the Clarendon Centre, Oxford involved the whole class.

showing how many of which items they would need for the trip.

In planning this trip the children had had to identify the problems and calculate the capacity of the bus, the distance, the cost. They had had to make and complete a questionnaire of class needs. They had had to draw conclusions ('We'll have to go twice'), give reasons ('Diesel is cheaper'), quote sources of evidence ('My dad says'), ask questions to clarify ('What'll it cost?'), ask questions for points of information ('Who can we ask?') and to direct attention to issues ('What about lunch?'). They had also predicted ('The driver should know'), empathised ('You can't disturb him, it's not fair'), used analogies to support suggestions ('We always use maps on holiday'), compromised and taken decisions about food ('OK, we'll have to ask everyone') and collaborated through listening and contributing throughout.

By the end of their first year, they were already remarkably competent in discussion skills. These skills had been modelled to them by their teacher, they had practised the skills, and they were now able to use them in groups on their own. However, they were not yet at a stage where they found it easy to make that knowledge explicit.

However, by the time children become top infants many can be explicit concerning their own and others' discussion skills. They can also prove to be highly committed to discussion as a means of planning and decision-making, especially regarding issues which are of vital concern to themselves.

An example from a class of six- and seven-year-olds serves to illustrate how awareness of discussion strategies can lead to the development of those strategies. Such top infant children can be very accomplished as participants in discussions. They can recognise the importance of turn-taking, of listening to each other to get ideas, of giving clear instructions and explanations, of putting their own views with evidence or justification where necessary if an issue is in dispute, as well as the importance of asking others to explain or elaborate if they have not understood a point made previously, and also of hypothesising and evaluating.

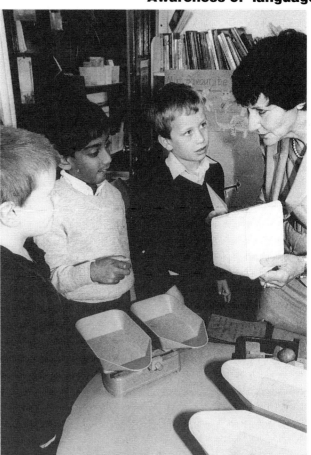

Teacher participation is still very valuable and important in maintaining 'discourse conventions'.

However, a teacher's presence can still be an important factor in maintaining such 'discourse conventions'. Frequently, because the discussions involve issues which are of real concern to the children, they can still get carried away because of the excitement which these discussions can generate.

The children found that being an active contributor was less of a problem than being an active listener. They found it more difficult to listen to each other, to understand what was meant, to recognise the implications, to discriminate between what they agreed with and what they didn't, between what was sound and what wasn't and, finally, to offer constructive and critical comment in a way which the recipient would find easy to consider.

This need to be a 'critical listener' had already emerged in the context of response partners for story-telling. In this context the children, together with the teacher, had established a 'code of conduct':

- Listen carefully and follow the story,
- Think of two good things to say,
- Ask if something wasn't very clear to you,
- Suggest something which you think might make it better.

Such strategies for 'critical listening' were already being put into use during the writing group discussions. The class and teacher later extended such an approach to discussions in general.

An opportunity to make explicit their knowledge about language strategies in discussions emerged as a result of an abortive argument when feelings had run high. The children were asked if the discussion had been useful. The unanimous verdict was 'No'. In trying to identify why, a very interesting discussion did in fact emerge. This was extended to the whole class and a list of criteria concerning what makes a good discussion was suggested by the children. The children decided that it was best to write them down in the order in which they thought they would actually happen during the discussion. The final list was:

- Explain well,
- Listen to other people,
- Take turns to talk,
- Wait until the other person finishes,
- Say things which help other people,
- Keep to the subject,
- Share ideas with the rest of the group,
- Give suggestions and ideas,
- Be careful how you say things so that other people don't get upset,
- Ask each other questions so as to make things clear,
- Sort and test ideas,
- Choose ideas together,
- Try not to be bossy in the group,

Having decided what they ought to do in a discussion (the aims) the children then moved on to thinking up how they could get better at doing any of these things (the strategies). Different pairs of children undertook to write down some tips to help people. Each tip was written on a card and then all the tips relating to one of the criteria were contained in a plastic zip-bag.

The criteria were typed in a list form and photocopied. Before each group

discussion the children were asked to look at their list and to identify any particular criteria which they felt they needed to work on. They could go to the zip-bags and read the tip cards, if they wanted any suggestions for developing that particular skill. For example to explain well:

- Wait till everybody is listening,
- Make things clear,
- Ask a friend for advice,
- Make notes to help you to remember,
- Put your ideas in order,
- Speak well so other people can hear,
- Choose your words carefully so others can understand.

To listen to others:

- Ask someone to talk to you,
- Try to understand what they say,
- Remember what they say,
- Look at the person who is speaking,
- Make sure everyone is quiet.

Not all the criteria were given such detailed treatment. Nevertheless, discussing the criteria in pairs, choosing strategies, then presenting these to the rest of the class

Children find it more difficult to be an active listener than an active contributor.

In groups, children can practise and assess their discussion skills.

resulted in the fact that many important skills were identified and brought to the children's attention. These skills so often remain implicit, assumed, and unarticulated, and they are the ones which children (and adults) often find hard to become aware of, let alone to put into practice.

At the end of the group task the children were given time (sometimes 20 minutes) to reflect upon their discussion and in particular upon the criteria they had selected for special attention. At first this proved very difficult to do. However, the children soon became more proficient at those skills, and also more proficient at the delicate task of assessing each other and accepting the assessment given to them. Gradually, some ground rules emerged to make the process easier, for example, 'always try to comment about something someone was good at first'.

Further significant issues were discussed which raised questions about the validity of monitoring individuals whose performance depends on the group situation. In particular, how could the group assess someone's focus criteria if that strategy hadn't been demanded of them during the discussion? How could the group assess a member's progress in 'asking each other questions to make things clear' if they had not needed to do this because the others were explaining things so clearly?

The children had become acutely aware of some of the key skills and attitudes needed when contributing in such discussions. They also began to notice them in other classroom situations. For instance, a helping adult was joining in an art activity and a group member commented, appropriately, 'you were saying things to help other people'. Phrases such as 'keep to the subject' and 'that was a nice thing you said' became common in class even outside the specific context of group work and without any reminders of collaborative working techniques.

This awareness extended to activities outside the classroom as well. For example, just after playtime, the children in a group were asked to select their focus criteria when one of the group remarked 'I know why we didn't have a good game today...I didn't listen to what the others wanted'. It seemed therefore that the children were beginning to transfer their awareness of positive group discussion strategies to situations in the playground too.

The approach to discussion skills described involved the children at every step. It was they who recognised that earlier discussions had not been constructive. It was they who began to identify the reasons for this and what might be done to improve discussions. It was the children who decided the criteria, in their own terms, and who initially chose to mark themselves in order to see if they were getting better. Identifying the skills was itself a considerable achievement. But learning to implement them and then to expose themselves to peer assessment made heavy demands on their maturity. Yet in the space of a term these top infants showed themselves well-able to make an impressive start on exercising these very elusive skills explicitly.

The children were quite able to communicate effectively in an oral mode, to 'reflect upon and adjust their language' in order to 'facilitate their own and other's comprehension'.

Interest and value in knowledge about language

Ruth Weir's account of her child (1970) shows that babies play with sounds in their cribs and enjoy the feel of sounds in their mouths. This marks the beginning of what is often a lifelong fascination with words, a natural curiosity about language which teachers can encourage and support.

It seems appropriate to begin with the language children use amongst themselves for social and learning purposes, and to exploit their spontaneous interest.

Forms, functions and features of language

Surface features: sounds and spelling

Children's awareness of and pleasure in language grows continually. For example, reception children frequently enjoy making up words - often to insult each other but also for the pleasure in experimenting! An adult in the 'home corner' would not be surprised to overhear exchanges like the following one:

'"You're a pooh-pooh."
"You're a soo-soo."
"You're a silly-billy."
"You're a willy-wally."'

Usually such 'games' are conducted in a friendly fashion. The techniques employed often rely on doubling word sounds or rhyming them. It is a feature of children's pleasure in words which is employed in choosing character's names in many stories for children of this age, eg Henny-Penny, or Dame Wishy-Washy.

A group of six-year-olds found another game which involved playing with surface features of words. They were fascinated when one of them noticed that they could spell their names backwards, sometimes making an alternative word, sometimes making something that was merely pronounceable: so Mrs Tan became Mrs Nat, Lee became Eel, Ben became Neb, Carol became Laroc and, to the delight of all, Miss Armitage became Miss Egatimra. For about a week some of the children talked

backwards to each other and wrote backwards letters, until the novelty wore off. But it certainly generated an enthusiasm for playing with surface features of words as a game in itself and led to investigating palindromes such as 'dad', 'toot', and 'madam'.

Despite the wealth of insight which can be derived from the spoken word it is often through discussion of written texts that we can more easily reflect upon words. Talking about words, not just with words, leads to the developing of what Olson (1984) calls the literate person who 'is aware of language as an artefact' that one can study as well as use.

Listening to poetry in particular provides tremendous pleasure in the word games, melody and sound effects it can create. Stories also provide a wealth of features to discuss - from identifying new words and finding strategies for trying to pronounce them (such as recognising letter strings and syllables as in Attainment

Playground games develop children's awareness of language.

Target 4, Key Stage 2), to finding prefix/ suffix patterns (AT 3/4, Key Stage 2), to noting similar/dissimilar aural and visual patterns (such as in homographs and homophones and their role in puns suggested in Attainment Targets 2-4, Key Stage 2), all of which leads to a heightened awareness of word structures.

Word structures

Other discoveries made when top infants were exploring words can be seen in the following incidents. A group of six-year-olds noticed some of their names could be divided into separate words:

Stephen = step + hen

Justin = just + tin

Having explored more of these a girl enquired, 'Do we call it an ''outing'' because we go out and then come back in again?'!

This developed into an interest in word compounds, although the specialist term in this instance wasn't introduced. Children used the term 'word sums' and made up examples for each other. Some of these were examples where each of the components were known words, and they formed a new word which was a sum of the meanings of the parts, for example:

school + boy =

On other occasions the final word bore no relationship to the meanings of its components, for example:

car + pet =

Other compounds were introduced where the components were known but the compound wasn't, for example:

handy + man =

A variation of this game, which directed attention to surface features, was a form of the traditional parlour game where competitors try to make as many words out of the constituent letters of a given word.

One seven-year-old child called this 'finding the "locked in" words', for example:

cupboard = cup, up, board, oar

or by choosing non-consecutive letters, pod, cub, rod, rap etc.

Word-building took a different form with a group of nine-year-old children. This time the children had been on an outing to a local complex of buildings which included a church and quadrangle. Interest was shown, as can be seen in the following questions:

'Is a quadrangle like a triangle?'

'No, silly. Triangles have got three something. Like tricycles.'

'So what's a quadrangle then?'

'Like quads, when you have lots of babies.'

'How many?'

'Lots!'

This led to the exploration of words beginning with uni, bi, (du), tri, quad etc. Children discussed the 'one-ish-ness' about 'universe' or 'Manchester United' or 'uniform'. They also found science fiction terms from TV programmes which included 'a uni-quad-mobile' which, I was told, is 'a car for one person which has four wheels and it goes on the moon'. Such investigations which focused on roots and derivations led to considerable searching for explanations of how new words are invented. The children found advertising a constant source of ideas. In this instance, the children used terms to describe the different processes, such as 'add-ons', 'melting words into each other', 'crazy spellings'.

The fact that words were invented by people rather than just somehow 'existing' was a novel idea and led to frequent questioning about why a table is called a table and so on. Origins of onomatopoeic words were more easily recognised. Comics provided a good source of action words and words which show noises. The fact that in comics words actually 'show' their meanings in the calligraphy led to further investigations of calligrams, typefaces and, later, differences in letter shapes in different historical periods and in the scripts of different cultures - another aspect where

surface features can sometimes be found to have originated in a close relationship of signifier (graphic symbol, or letter shape) and its referent (that abstract or concrete object to which it refers).

Acquisition of language

Primary-aged children very often have younger siblings or cousins who may be at the age when they are learning to talk. Such younger relatives can also be a language resource. Children are able to bring into school examples of babies' talk, as well as the 'baby talk' adults indulge in when talking to babies. School-aged children are adept at understanding their younger sibling's talk (as well as what their doting elders mean), and can usually expand the telegraphic sentences into the structures which reflect how they would say things themselves. This can result in the children constructing sentences quite naturally, and providing comparative structures which they can discuss and which can lead them towards articulating 'what makes them different'. By such a process they make a beginning at finding out how children learn language, developing their own working definition for a 'sentence', and starting to consider models for developing younger children's language.

A class of junior children also considered the situation of a newcomer to the school for whom English was not their mother-tongue. The question 'What English do they need most when they come to school?' generated a range of suggestions. It also raised questions like, 'How could you teach someone a new language?' and 'Do children learn in the same way as babies?'.

The majority of suggestions for a 'basic English' resulted in a list of isolated words of a very school-specific nature, eg a list of all the teachers' names, the new child's name, yes, no, hallo, goodbye, toilet, help, and a list of every sport or playground activity that a newcomer might be likely to want to join. Such an approach was challenged by others in the class: 'That's not how people talk... you should teach them the proper way first'. When the usefulness of single words was challenged it was defended: 'You just put words together if you want to'.

In order to make it easy to learn, ideas ranged from memorising items in order of likely need, to arranging contrasting pairs of words with picture clues which were funny 'because it's easier to learn funny things' such as:
tennis racket, cricket bat; descant recorder, tape recorder; swimming trunks, elephant trunks.

Another group, however, began with what they believed were basic sentences to meet basic needs. This was followed by

A class of junior children made a list of basic words for a newcomer to the school for whom English was not their mother-tongue.

152

trying to think how these might be taught. Initially the sentences were grouped in sets which 'went together' in terms of meanings. One child noticed that some of the sentences made a pattern which resulted in regrouping 'because it would be easy to learn them if they are nearly the same':

May I have the skipping rope?
May I have the rubber?
May I borrow the glue?
May I go and change my book?
Can I join?
Can I play with the polygons?

Shall I use colour pencils?
Where is the paper?
When shall I open my eyes?
What happens now?
How do I do this?

Sorry, I didn't mean to.
Please don't do that.
I don't understand.
Thank you for letting me play.

This led to questions concerning the different between 'may I?', 'can I?'and 'shall I?'. It was also noted that most of the sentences on the basic list were in the form of questions. Some pointed out that asking the question was one thing, but what about understanding the answer...? In addition, it was not felt that a newcomer would need to answer other people's questions 'because they can see what you are doing, whether you're stuck, whether you like it...'.

Such considerations formed the beginnings of a growing awareness of the skills of children who spoke more than one language, a respect for their achievement, and greater sympathy with the frustrations of trying to learn a new language in the busy classroom.

These discussions did not lead to much specialist vocabulary. Instead the forms were discussed in terms of their functions, particularly their social functions and the degrees of 'politeness' needed in order to get what you want. This would be in keeping with Donaldson's assertion (1989) that 'children are concerned with what people mean, not with what words mean'.

Games involve a wealth of different types of language.

Language varieties: generational, geographical, historical

Playground talk

Children have a very rich resource in their own language which they use among themselves, particularly in the playground. This embraces both the oral traditions of rhymes and chants that the Opies have recorded so extensively, and the rapidly-changing slang of the playground, where superlatives and approbations are a central part of everyday life, even if they are not common everyday language elsewhere. In the area of 'oral traditions' children show themselves to be excellent guardians of continuity. However, in the area of superlatives the children show themselves to be particularly creative in the terms which they invent. Fashions come and go rapidly. What was 'great' becomes 'brill', then 'bad', 'wicked' (even 'well-wicked'), perhaps even 'crucial' or 'storming'. Trying to decide the continuum of such 'in' words, their origins, how they are formed or extended, can give rise to heated debate which generates a new more explicit appreciation of forms and nuance.

Nuance was also the key to another form of continuum which came under scrutiny. In trying to describe friends, family or people you know, sensitivity to the connotations of word pairs (antonyms) such as fat-thin, ugly-handsome, thick-clever, nice-nasty became very important. So 'word slides' were devised. This was easier if the words related to physical attributes:

'ginormous, giant, blubbery, big, podgy, porky, large' or 'slim, skinny, thin'.

However, these slides frequently included words which moved from the denotative to the connotative:

'muscle, strong, weak, dumb...'

The task became more difficult still if the words were related to personality rather than physical attributes. The word slides generated synonyms which demarcated the semantic field of each word in the word-pair rather than indicating the gradations of meaning between them:

'nice, kind, loving, grateful, laughing, surprising'; 'nasty, horrible, spiteful, wicked, mean, hateful'.

This kind of investigation into children's own language can easily lead into a consideration of what kind of talk parents and grandparents used at the same age. Further, where there is a mobile school population where parents change jobs and move house there may be the opportunity

Children love to investigate 'fashionable' words that they use.

for children to contribute dialect words from their different localities. Even in an area of static population, children are exposed to language varieties through a wide range of TV programmes and presenters. There are also plenty of differences between Australian English, American English which children can analyse and study (and there are plenty of viewers of *Neighbours* and *Dallas*!).

Geographical and historical varieties

Moving from the playground to the family can provide an interesting source of words are remarkably similar across a wide range of Indo-European languages, and also Slavonic languages - from Hindi to Russian to German to English, Irish and Welsh.

Sanskrit	English
pitar	father
matar	mother
brahtar	brother
svasar	sister

Latin	Welsh
pater	tad
mater	mam
frater	brawd
soror	chwaer

Russian	Irish
papa	athair
mama	mathair
brat	brathair
siestra	

German
vater
mutter
bruder
schwester

Words related to numerals also show a remarkable similarity.

Latin

unus	sex
duo	septum
tres	octo
quattuor	novem
quinque	decem

Spanish	Sanskrit
uno	eka
dos	dvau
tres	tri
cuatro	catvara
cinco	panca
seis	shat
siete	sapta
ocho	ashtau
nueve	nava
diez	dasha

English	Bengali
one	ekh
two	dui
three	tin
four	cha
five	panch
six	choi
seven	shaat
eight	aat
nine	noi
ten	dosh

German	Hindi/Urdu
eins	ek
zwei	do
drei	tin
vier	char
funf	panch
sechs	chai
seiban	sat
acht	ath
neun	nau
zehn	das

Examining these patterns could perhaps help children to develop a 'civilised respect' for other languages which are so like their own.

Another resource from within the family are the names; both 'family' or surnames and 'personal' or first names. These too have meanings which can be explored, and fashion trends which can be monitored. Nicknames, celebrity names, book character names are all 'labels' which can be investigated and speculated upon.

Moving outside the school playground, into the High Street, there is further evidence of language varieties. Loan words such as 'launderette', 'restaurant', 'menu', 'kebab','pizza', 'anorak', 'sputnik' or 'shampoo' may be a surprise to children - though some are easy for children to spot by their 'un-English' spelling strings, (particularly the endings) or sometimes by their pronounciation. When and why these particular words were incorporated into English is a matter upon which children can speculate. What English words other languages borrow, and why, can also be suggested.

Beyond the High Street, there are of course place names which can be an enormous resource for investigating meanings and patterns of distribution. Any of these foci can serve to heighten the fact that words can be created, combined, changed to communicate changing needs: that words are made by human beings to serve a purpose, they are put together in particular ways to help others to understand what we choose to say, that language is both created and creative. The ultimate, of course, is to embark on creating your own code or language. Children often do this spontaneously in their friendship groups, or gangs. 'Secret languages' are a sign of belonging, of membership.

Playing with words

Words are 'weird and wonderful things' and an endless source of fascination for many children. By the age of about eight, many children are likely to be ready to stand back and to look at words rather than be totally absorbed in using them. The lower junior age is often a period when children really enjoy puns and jokes and become very adept at manipulating words cleverly. This is not to say that younger children don't also do this. But the play is often of a different type.

Perera (1987) illustrates another feature of children's ability to play, not only with word sounds, but also with associations and meanings. She quotes an example of a five-year-old making a model

The High Street provides further evidence of language varieties.

of Guy Fawkes. His friend made another model and announced, 'I'm going to call mine knife - they'll be Knife and Fawkes!' Here are children enjoying a good joke, playing with word associations.

Asking children to make their own joke books doesn't usually require much encouragement. Asking them also to collect jokes from younger children in the school can lead to trying to work out what makes a joke funny and whether children tell different kinds of jokes at different ages.

The jokes which the children collect can, very tentatively, be classified to demonstrate different linguistic awareness at different ages. The jokes show children 'playing' with different aspects of language.

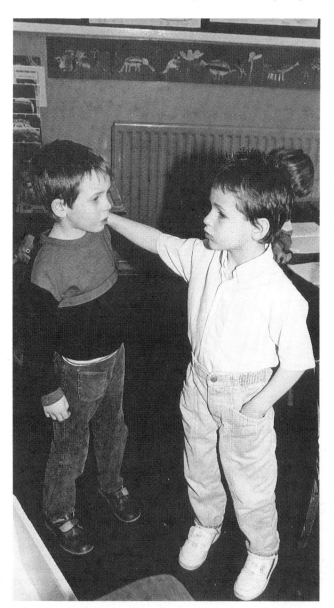

Jokes are a useful source to encourage use of language.

For example:

- Sounds/sense/surface features (nonsense, puns, spellings)
What do you get if cross a cow with a duck?
...a cream quacker. (Five-year-old)
What do vampire doctors say to their patients?
...'Necks, please'. (Seven-year-old)
What do you do to make a witch itch?
...take away her 'w'. (Nine-year-old)
- Situations (literal, lateral, logical)
Why do witches fly on broom sticks?
...because Hoovers are too heavy. (Six-year-old)
Why did the policeman cry?
...because he wanted to take his Panda to bed. (Eight-year-old)
What gets bigger the more you take from it?
...a hole. (Eight-year-old)
- Structural (word boundaries, pronoun references, phrase modifiers)
'Knock, knock,' 'Who's there?' 'Justin.' 'Justin who?' 'Just in time for tea.' (Seven-year-old)
Teacher on phone: 'Hallo, I hear Jimmy is ill and can't come to school. To whom am I speaking?'
Voice: 'This is my father...' (Ten-year-old)
'I got out of bed, grabbed a gun and shot the lion in my pyjamas!'
...'What was the lion doing in your pyjamas?' (Ten-year-old)
- There are plenty of sick jokes, political jokes, and currently topical jokes which are among the growing repertoire of older juniors:
Why did Michael Jackson call his latest album 'Bad'?
...Because he didn't know how to spell 'pathetic'. (Nine-year-old)
- And then there are jokes about jokes, which rely on the participants taking one step further back in their awareness of the games language plays...
'Waiter, waiter, there's a frog in my soup.'
...'The fly is on holiday.' (Nine-year-old).

In fact, there appeared to be a 'spiral curriculum' of developing awareness about and knowledge of language which grew with age. The language skills were constantly changing, even though many of the jokes were old!

Awareness, analysis and appreciation of English

Increasing children's awareness of spoken language can be an important step towards increasing their valuation of their own and other people's languages in all their glorious varieties. The programmes of study and attainment targets in the National Curriculum are based on the assumption that making explicit the implicit understandings that children already have will enable them to realise their entitlement to language in terms of their increased pleasure in and improved use of English.

The National Curriculum also outlines a range of knowledge which it is believed children need to acquire. Knowledge about oracy is given equal weight, for the first time, with literacy. This knowledge extends to knowledge about how children use talk for different purposes (eg presentational, interactional or in play and drama), for different audiences (eg peer, teacher, other adults). It particularly relates to styles of delivery, and being able to adjust talk in the processes of discussion, problem-solving, or planning. Using talk for learning, especially in collaborative situations, also entails a particular attitude to the value of talk and the value of the collaborative context.

In addition, encouragement to share reading and writing with peers and adults could lead to an increase in opportunities for talking about and studying the meanings of texts and words, which can both enhance our understanding of the literary texts and the language they use, and can expand and enrich our own oral language too.

Furthermore, encouraging the use of children's talk as the basis for investigation - whether playground talk, playing with talk, talking about word play, talking about different ways of talking - can contribute to an increasing ability to analyse, to be aware of, and to appreciate the richness of oral language.

Appendix

References

Class, Codes and Control, B Bernstein (Routledge and Kegan Paul)

Talking about Mathematics, T Brissenden (Blackwell)

A Language for Life (The Bullock Report), DES (HMSO)

Mathematics for Ages 5 - 16, DES (HMSO)

Science for Ages 5 - 16, DES (HMSO)

English for Ages 5 - 11, DES (HMSO)

English for Ages 5 - 16, DES (HMSO)

Common Knowledge, D Edwards and N Mercer (Methuen)

Inside the Primary Classroom, M Galton B Simon, and P Croll (Routledge and Kegan Paul)

All our Languages, D Houlton (Edward Arnold)

Children and Number, M Hughes (Blackwell)

Language in the Inner City, W Labov (Blackwell)

Linguistic Minorities in England: Summary Report, Linguistic Minorities Project, London Institute of Education

Maths Talk, Mathematical Association, (Stanley Thornes)

Oracy Matters, M Maclure, T Phillips and A Wilkinson (Open University Press)

Teaching the Universe of Discourse, J Moffett (Houghton Mifflin)

Every Child's Language, Open University, Multilingual Matters

The Lore and Language of Schoolchildren, I Opie and P Opie (Oxford University Press)

Educational Linguistics, M Stubbs (Basil Blackwell)

'Research and Practice in the Primary Classroom', S Tann in *Grouping and Group Work*, ed by B Simon and J Willcocks , (Routledge and Kegan Paul)

Young Children Learning, B Tizard and M Hughes (Fontana)

Language Perspectives, B Wade (Heinemann)

Talking to Some Purpose, B Wade (Educational Review Publications)

Reading for Real, B Wade (Open University Press)

'Children becoming pupils: a study of discourse in nursery and reception classes', M Willes in *Uttering Muttering* ed by C Adelman (Grant McIntyre)

Teaching Information Skills through Project Work, D Wray (Hodder & Stoughton)

Project Teaching, D Wray (Scholastic Publications)

About the authors

David Wray

David Wray, general editor and author for this Teacher Handbook, is a lecturer in primary education at the University of Exeter. Prior to this he was a lecturer at University College, Cardiff, having taught for several years in primary schools, before moving into teacher education. He has edited two collections about using the micro and reading for the United Kingdon Reading Association, as well as writing several other books and articles, including *Bright Ideas Writing* and *Project Teaching* (Management Books series), both published by Scholastic Publications.

Sarah Tann

Barrie Wade

Barrie Wade has taught in primary and secondary schools and is now Senior Lecturer in Education at the University of Birmingham. He is editor of *Educational Review* and has published a number of educational books, for example, *Story at Home and School*, (University of Birmingham), *Talking to Some Purpose*, (University of Birmingham) and *Reading for Real*, (Open University Press), as well as numerous articles in journals. He also writes prose and peotry for adults and children. His latest poetry for children is *Conkers* (Oxford University Press), and André Deutsch will shortly publish a picture book, *Little Monster*.

Sarah Tann

Sarah Tann is currently Reader in Education at Oxford Polytechnic. She is now involved in primary teacher training, having previously worked on classroom research programmes and taught in nursery, primary and middle schools.

Terry Phillips

Terry Phillips is a lecturer in education in the School of Education, University of East Anglia. Before becoming a lecturer he taught in junior (7 - 11) and primary (5 - 11) schools, in London, and in a Wiltshire primary school where he was deputy head. He has also been a teacher-tutor in a Norwich (8 - 12) middle school. Whilst in Australia for a year as visiting lecturer at a college of advanced education, he taught part-time in a two-teacher bush school. He finds it increasingly difficult to draw a line

Terry Phillips

involving children in their own learning and thus in the value of talk for real purposes.

Clive Carré

Clive Carré is Senior Lecturer at the University of Exeter, School of Education. He graduated in biology at Bristol University and subsequently undertook research in animal physiology at the University of Sydney. He has taught science at primary and secondary levels. He has written a number of books and articles on science education, including *Language Teaching & Learning Science* (Ward Lock Education Series). He visits Canada regularly and contributes each year to a Language and Learning Masters programme. He has been a language consultant for *Science Plus* (Harcourt Brace Jovanovich, Canada), a series of junior high science texts. His current research interest is in teacher education for primary teachers.

Clive Carré

between teaching, learning and research having discovered that research is the unavoidable consequence of all good teaching. Since he started teaching Terry has researched into primary children's oral response to literature, small group discussion in the classroom and the relationship between group talk and modes of thinking. He now devotes much of his time to supporting school teachers and health professional teachers as they enquire into the processes of communication in their own classrooms.

Terry has been a member of NATEs primary and middle years committees and is currently a member of their publications committee.

Margaret Armitage

Margaret Armitage has just taken up a headship in a rural village primary school near Oxford. She has taught 5 - 8 year olds for 18 years and is now teaching 9 - 11 year olds. A six week secondment and an external correspondence course heightened her awareness of the importance of

Janet Duffin

Janet Duffin was a secondary teacher of mathematics before going into teacher training, first at the Kingston- upon- Hull College of Education (later incorporated into the Humberside College of Higher Education) and then in the Department of Educational Studies at the University of Hull. She did a period of work in the Kingston- upon -Hull Child Guidance Clinic where was interested in learning problems in both reading and mathematics. She has run in-service courses for teachers in problem solving and contributed to courses nationwide on language and talk in mathematics. For the past five years she has worked in the Language Teaching Centre of the University of Hull, helping overseas students to learn English for academic purposes. Janet is also currently running courses for arts undergraduates in the Ernst & Whinney Numeracy Centre in the School of Mathematics at the University of Hull. These courses are designed to help the students improve and bring numeracy skills up-to-date in preparation for employment. She has written on aspects of problem solving and language in several journals for primary and secondary teachers as well as contributing a language component to a book on primary mathematics. During the past two and a half years she has acted as Evaluator of the CAN (Calculator Aware Number) component of the PrIME (Primary Initiatives in Mathematics Education). The findings of the CAN project, and the research into mathematics education that it opens up for the future, form an apt culmination to a life's work in mathematics teaching which has always had strong language connections.

Index

E

F

G

H

homographs, 149-50
homophones, 149-50
Hughes, M., 143
hypothesis, 18, 69-70, 145
    in project work, 81, 85

I

ILEA (Inner London Educational Authority), 27, 55
imagination, 16, 47, 70, 110, 113
imitation, 12, 53
immigration, 28
independence, 51, 80, 84, 117-18
initiative, 12, 86
'in talk', 140-1
interdependence, 51
interviews, 14, 19, 50, 68, 81
    in cross-curricular project, 18-19
    and language register, 32-3
    in science, 117-18
intonation, 52, 61
investigation, 50, 89, 144, 151
    and language varieties, 154-156
    in project work, 81, 83, 84
    in science, 48, 113
    and talk, 78, 158
Irish, 155
Italian, 28

J

jingles, 52, 55
jokes, 156-7

K

Kingman Report, 138-41

L

Labov, W, 35-6
Lancashire, 28
language
    acquisition, 138, 151-3
    appreciation, 39
    appropriate, 12, 19, 33-34, 61, 66
    of argument and reasoning, 66
    changes, 34

to clarify, 16, 17-18
codes, 35
command of, 34-5
compensation programmes, 35-6
competence, 37, 39
'correct', 33, 39
curiosity about, 149
deprivation, 34-6
development, 17, 26, 28, 55-6, 81, 127
discoveries, 111
effective use of, 34
environment, 36, 37, 140
to explore a role, 16
formal, 128
form and function, 138, 149-50
heritage, 140
and identity, 34, 36
for information, 16
and intellectual development, 109
interpretation of, 14
knowledge about, 138-141
learning, 12, 16, 33, 76, 140, 152
and listening, 44
manipulative, 142
in mathematics, 128, 134
in project work, 83, 92
purposes, 14-16, 65-6, 139-40, 149
reciprocity, 14-15
as resource, 37-39
respect for children's, 37, 39
rules, 138, 140
in science, 109, 111-12, 115, 118-19, 121
'secret', 139, 156
social context, 10, 28, 32-3
structure, 17, 27, 36
superior, 33-4
systems, 140
technical, 139
transactional, 6, 139
value of, 140
variation, 6, 26-39, 138-40
varieties, 153-6
see also awareness
language census (ILEA), 27
languages, 26-8, 35-9, 139, 153
    'civilised respect' for, 155
    Indo-European, 155
    and language awareness, 143
    learning, 42
    Slavonic, 155
    see also individual languages
language system, 11

S

T